Crash Course on Sex for Christian Couples

Crash Course Series, Volume 1

S. S. Thabethe

Published by S. S. Thabethe, 2023.

CRASH COURSE ON SEX FOR CHRISTIAN COUPLES

First edition. August 31, 2023.

Copyright © 2023 S. S. Thabethe.

ISBN: 979-8223546573

Written by S. S. Thabethe.

Dedication

This is book is dedicated to my wife, Banele Thabethe. You have won my heart, and you have given me a glimpse of the love Christ has for his bride- the Church. Thank you for putting up with an imperfect husband and for allowing me to write, even though it meant staying in bed alone at times. Thank you for your contribution to this book- words cannot describe my gratitude for you. To my son, don't read this until you're married, or shortly before. To my unborn children, listen to your older brother. To my friends and relatives- yes, I wrote a book about sex. To the Lord Jesus Christ, thank you for blessing me with such a wonderful life. Lastly, in memory of my late father, Dr. B. M. Thabethe (PhD) and my beloved uncle, Mr. L. R. P. Thabethe, I thank God for blessing me with the wisdom and love from these men who shaped my view of what it is to be a family man and their candour about their mistakes.

- SST

Disclaimer

The content contained in this book is solely the ideas of Samkele Sibusiso Thabethe, Sr. [the author] concerning the subject matter discussed. Views and opinions presented are not those of current nor former employers, associates or affiliated organisations.

The content contained in this book is the intellectual property of the author. You may not reuse, republish or reprint such content without written consent from the author. The content in this book is for information purposes. It is not intended as a substitute for professional marriage, medical or psychological advice. Should you decide to act upon any information in this book, you do so at your own risk.

While the information in this book has been verified to the best of the author's abilities, the author cannot guarantee that there are no mistakes or errors.

Introduction

Crash course

Noun [C][1]

UK /ˈkræʃ ˌkɔːs/ **US** /ˈkræʃ ˌkɔːrs/

A course that teaches you a lot of basic facts in a very short time (Cambridge Dictionary, 2023)

I was sitting on an inflatable bed one morning while visiting my sister-in-law and her husband at their house. The year 2022 was nearing its end, and I had wondered what life would be like for me in the New Year. A review of life and marriage ensued and I was soon evaluating my life, my sex life in-particular. I pondered how little we see and hear about sex in the context of Christian marriage and how bombarded we are about sex and sexuality in the mainstream media... after all, *sex sells*. But what drew me to this was a curiosity about understanding what makes sex so desirable, and what makes satisfaction in this area so elusive. I also wondered why there was so much infidelity and divorce. Could there be a connection between these things, or was I simply spinning in my mind?

It was this conversation that took place in my head that would usher the birth of this book. Over the following day my mind would be consumed by the desire to explore the subject further. Several weeks into this all-consuming train-of-thought led to an outline, then a few words which have now become a book. I would also get an encounter with a group of young men attending a Christian version of a bachelor party, where a discussion about sex before marriage came up, and one contributor to this discussion indicating that he will have questions for God in *Heaven*, chiefly; why did he equip us with the tools for sex and then prohibit us from using them before marriage (more on this conversation in *Chapter 1*).

---

1. https://dictionary.cambridge.org/help/codes.html

When I got married, I had two objectives in mind. The first, was to stay married till I die. This came off of my parents' divorce, the difficulties they experienced and my own challenges in navigating their separation. I never wanted my children to experience what I went through, but most of all, I never wanted to go through the pain my parents experienced. Though I can only imagine what the separation was like for them, the imagination is enough to make the whole thing completely undesirable for me.

The second objective was to enjoy being married. This was something borne out of the mismatch between classical romance literature and the status quo in marriages around me. Hollywood is a great reflection of pop-culture, and Hollywood's portrayal of marriage conveys a bleak picture on enduring romances. When you watch movies like *The Notebook*[1], you cannot help but wonder if love like that still exists. I quit wondering, and set out to create a love better than that. It is not easy, but it is attainable. But one of the areas where I had to succeed in order to realise this dream was **SEX.**

Among other things, I had to have a great sex life with my wife in order to achieve this dream. This is when I began reading tons of material about sex. In the mind of a complete Christian virgin, sex ahead of your wedding can be very daunting- you *can't* ask a lot of people about the topic, especially Christians. You can hardly read a book about sex openly unless you want to be excommunicated from the faith (hence my preference for e-books in this area, bless the Lord!). You can hardly watch anything without having your purity violated or your righteousness under question. Your last resort is to pray, and hope that the Lord grants you the know-how in the moment. It was in this moment when I wished there was someone who would give me a run-down on sex while protecting my purity, righteousness and understanding of what it is to be Christian.

Why a Crash Course

I used to think that men absolutely loved sex and women tolerated it for their sake. Don't ask me why, I'm entitled to a dose of unreasonable silliness. My wife taught me something amazing to change this view, she asked me "why would God make you (a man) a helper (wife) that is not suitable for your desire which occurs naturally for you?" I was changed. I discovered then that the issue is rarely a lack of desire for the sake of a lack of desire. The lack of sexual desire for each other in a marriage is often a symptom of something else, typically a mismatch of interests or an imbalance in the satisfaction of needs.

The aim of this book is to answer the prayer of the version of myself months before my wedding. I want to give a concise account of what sex is, how to go about it and shed some light on a number of things within the topic of sex. As you may deduce from the latter statement, this will not be an exhaustive coverage on sex. The title is also telling in that I am giving a crash course. This is deliberate, because a couple's sexual relationship can never be the same as their neighbour's sexual relationship. We all make of our sex lives what we want, just like we do in our marriage relationship. Some of us are outgoing and adventurous while others prefer to be homebodies.

The other reason 'why a crash course' is because so much of the sex literature out there is confusing and seems out of reach. It is out of touch with the Christian mind-set and promotes promiscuity, fornication disguised as 'sexual liberty' and even adultery. There are also spiritual elements sprinkled on this literature that deviate from Biblical Christian faith. So if you don't want to take all of this literature *with a grain of salt*, this is a book for you. Speaking of a book for you, who might *you*[2] be?

Who is The Target Audience?

The book is written with my pre-marriage version of self in mind. So the ideal situation would be to read it when you're at that stage. However, the relevance of the material covered here seems to span across a lifetime. So regardless of where you are in your marriage journey, this is a book for you. Perhaps you want to re-ignite the spark (See Chapter 8), or you want some quick ideas to spice things up (See Chapter 9), or a quick run-down on sex positions (See Chapter 3)... this book is definitely for you. The assumption is that you have a biblical worldview and that you believe in heterosexual marriage. I would advise against reading this if you are not within months of getting married or already married- you don't want explosive ideas such as the ones I'm going to share floating about in your mind with no outlet... Please don't play with fire (see Proverbs 6:27).

What to Expect?

Not too much in the way of definitions. I want this book to be as to-the-point as possible. I also want you to get the lean bits you need to form your own sex life. I would recommend couples read this together for maximum results. It could serve as a great conversation starter, especially for couples in the pre-marital phase of their relationship. Otherwise, expect to absorb a lot over a short space of time. You can space this to your liking by adjusting you pace through the book. Like I do with my own reading, I tend to go back to specific parts for a refresher, and this might also help you.

Finally, expect candid coverage of a topic that has been taboo for so long. A bit of it might make you uncomfortable, but I hope the holistic experience enriches your life and makes for a solid foundation in your sex-life. If you're already having hot sex with your spouse, I hope this book helps you make it seven times hotter... (#Wink)

Another question you may have is why so many chapters for a book that is supposed to be concise? Isn't crash course supposed to be short? The answer is no, crash courses don't necessarily need to be short, the amount of information relative to the time is what makes a crash course a crash course. The other reason for this is that it is based on my preferences. I prefer to have a *Selah* moment when I read books the likes of this one. This is to allow myself to evaluate how I am doing in the area being covered, the possible changes I may want to make to improve, etc... I would like to afford you the same while making it easier for you to navigate back to different sections as a quick reference. In fact, I wrote the book with the aim of having it as a lifetime reference book on sex. However, you are welcome to consume the entire text in one go. Another heads-up that may be helpful is to note that the pace of the book changes for different sections; the tempo alters over the book so that at times you may feel like you're reading a summary, and in other instances you're reading an expository. This is also deliberate, as I respond to what the subject matter lends itself to.

Before journeying through this text, I'd like to pose a question to you; what is your ideal sex life? When we speak of a great sex life, what comes to mind? Is it the frequency of your sexual encounters with your spouse? Is it intensity of each sexual experience? Do you evaluate the greatness of sex over a longer term? Or is it fulfilling some of your naughtiest fantasies? Yes, you read that right... Naughty fantasies is being used in a 'for Christians' book. Anyways, I like to call an ideal sex life your *Sex Life Vision*.

Having a clearly defined *Sex Life Vision* will enable you to better articulate your sexual desires to your spouse. On the receiving end, it will help you understand your spouse's request better. It will help you avoid going through life with unresolved mismatches that frustrate you in the bedroom and outside of it.

Great Sex Fortifies Marriages

Great sex is such a multifaceted blessing. It boosts your confidence, improves sleep quality, maintains a great relationship with your spouse, and improves closeness and cognitive function. All these slow-down ageing, reduce stress, protects the brain and boosts self-esteem. I could go on, but the simple truth is that no one can say no to great sex. Then why is it an area of struggle? Why is there infidelity, divorce and a lack of confidence in the institution of marriage? Perhaps a read through these pages will help you understand the reasons for such devastating social ills and equip you with the tools to not only avoid these, but fortify your marriage from them.

One such means of fortification is what I call an *Accountability Sex-system*®. Great sex cannot happen outside of a great marriage and great marriage is not a one-man show. Having mentors or befriending other couples (as a couple) builds up your marriage. This is not a model I designed myself. I had attended an 11 year anniversary celebration planned by a friend of mine for him and his wife. One of the speakers at the celebration was a couple who had been married 43 years, and another 29 years. What I learnt from this was the importance of not walking the journey of marriage alone. None of the 'it's just me and you against the world' nonsense will do you any good in marriage. Interestingly, one of the couples shared an insight that I will walk with my whole life. They said it is important that you implement a system of relationship with 3 different couples in your marriage. A couple that is younger than you, older than you and a couple that's relatively the same 'age' as you. My takeaway is that age here refers to the number of years you have been married, i.e. if we have been married 5 years, a younger couple would be married 1 or 2 years, an older couple would be married for 30 years, and a couple relatively our 'age' would be 5 years.

The couple younger than you is important because they remind you where you have been and they reignite that kind of love you had for each other when it all began. There is something about the novelty of anything new; all just seems to click into place. This is important in keeping you revived. A younger couple will also keep you on your toes, causing you to watch your steps because another couple is learning from you.

A couple 'your age' will be good for talking about things that are relatable. It must be noted that the rate at which we achieve things in life is not the same, however our experiences may be similar as we go through identical stages in life, i.e. parenthood, career advancement, buying a house, car, etc... This is what this couple is for. In a weird sense, they are a good way to measure yourselves. Not to compare yourselves with envy, but to check whether the path you're leading is correct, more like a mirror. So choose wisely in this category.

The last of the three is the older couple. This is subject to personal preference. I wouldn't take a couple that has been married for 40 years when I am not even 5 years into my marriage. Somehow, their 40 year journey seems too out of reach for me. If you assess and see that their lifestyle and their ideas around marriage align to what and where you want to be, then by all means, build a relationship with them. This is not for me, contrarily, I favour a couple that has no more than 2 decades on me. At the time of writing, I am about 4 years into marriage, and we have a couple who are 11 years into their marriage, and

I think this is a reasonable gap for us. We also have a couple that has 17+ years in marriage, and they have a freshness about them that we like.

With this system in place, you can build your own accountability sex-system, even taking it to the level of discussing sex matters. This is important because our bodies change as we age, so some of the things you may encounter are experiences that the older couple may have gone through, and you can draw from this experience making your encounter less of a hassle than theirs.

So in reading this book, I want you to keep this in mind, and commit to reaching out to your accountability system concerning the insights you come across in this book. If you are benefitting from this work, why not extend the benefit to others? It will enhance your experience of this book, and will make your marriage better for it. I encourage you to send the link to this book and related material to 3 married couples and talk about it. My suggestion is that you tell them about your reading of this book, as this creates a situation where you're giving the other party the right to follow-up on how you're finding the book and what it is that you're applying from it. It also calls on you to be selective on who you involve in this accountability sex-system. The other aspect of this is the understanding that a system has many different parts that work together for the benefit of all parties involved, so choose wisely and let the Holy Spirit guide you in your choosing. Another key element to this is to connect with your spouse through reading of this book, both together and apart.

Facts about this Book and the Author

My worldview is biblical. I see things through the lens of what God has said in his word, the Bible. I am a Christian, this is being a follower of Christ Jesus. So that Christian, in the context of this book is not Protestant, Baptist, Catholic, or any other denomination or creed. In the context of this book, a Christian is anyone who accepts that Christ is God incarnate and that He was crucified for the sins of mankind. This is one who accepts Jesus Christ of Nazareth as documented in scripture and submits to His Lordship.

What you will notice is that I keep alternating between physical and non-physical elements of married sex. It almost seems like I am going back and forth; first it's sex and the mind, then sex positions, then back to fantasies, then the act of sex, then personal sexual history, then oral sex... this is by design as I want to underscore the importance of understanding the psychological and physiological reality of sex. I am not doing this as a medical professional, but as a person who has learnt that great sex begins in the mind and is manifested physically by use of our body parts. I have also learnt that conquering the mental/psychological elements of sex is 80% of the task of creating a blissful sex life.

Finally, as it pertains to facts, this is not a 'how to guide' on sex. Sure, there are some elements of it that can be considered a 'how-to' but in the main, it is not aimed at teaching you how. I am convinced that our biggest problems in sex are not 'how to?' problems. They tend to be 'why to' and 'what to' problems. For example, you're not feeling like you need more sex because you don't know how to have more sex... That's a simple enough problem to solve. But what you need to do in order to solve the issue is what plagues you. You're also not concerned about how your first night will go because you do not know how the dance of sexual intercourse goes. It's the other stuff that hides itself under our fears and doubts. We're also subconsciously concerned with the question of 'why to'? Why should we even engage in sexual intercourse, other than the pleasure it brings us on a physiological plane. If you pay attention, the answers to these and other questions will become apparent as you read through this book.

My Appeal to *you*

Most of us like the idea of learning new things- period. Putting these to action is something else entirely. When we read something that sparks our interest or exposes our blind spots, the reaction is usually *'I need to change that'* or *'I'd like to change that'* and we never take action. This is because we love the idea of doing *'good'*, because human beings are intrinsically good. Yet we rarely show the same enthusiasm in making the changes required for us to do *good* because change is not easy. This is why so many of us know exactly where we need improvement in our eating, exercise, finances and other areas- but we keep postponing the start date for change. Don't let this be you concerning your sex life. If you learn something in the pages to follow, harden not your heart and resolve to change. This is my appeal to you. Don't be ignorant and disregard the knowledge presented here, it is for a purpose that God has brought you into contact with this material and I believe it is my purpose to serve this book to you to enrich your marriage. Know this, it is not coincidental that you are reading this, make it count and make the changes for a better marriage.

Writing this book has been one of the most excruciatingly exciting experiences of my life. I enjoyed seeing it come together but I hated the pain of feeling guilty for going a day without adding anything to it. I remember writing some notes at a coffee chop, jumping out of a shower to take notes before they evade my mind and the times I woke from my sleep and dashed to my desk to take down what God had laid in my heart. However, while writing this book I also kept having visions of the reactions that some people in my circle would have when they found out I had wrote a book, especially one about a topic so taboo. Leaning into this thinking, I realised how cultured we have become that we sometimes get tempted to disregard the call that has been laid in our hearts by God on account of fear, fearing the ridicule that some among us would serve us when we tackle matters as difficult as sex. But the deeper question was why? Why did Christians have such an aversion to discussing matters of sex, even among married couples? My question was *Why is sex taboo for Christians?* You'd have to read the next chapter to see my findings.

Chapter 1: Why is Sex Taboo for Christians?

Materialism vs. Spiritualism

A Christian's mind is driven by a biblical understanding of the world and how he/she relates to it. There is nothing fundamentally wrong with this approach to life because as believers we are to be guided by God's word in how we do life. It is important to mention this fact before I go on because I do not want to create an impression of disregard for the authority of the Word. On the contrary, I want to clarify that the Word of God is and should be the ultimate authority of our lives[3].

The detachment between a Christian's life and what the Word determines to be an ideal life arises, in the words of one pastor, when we are 'too heavenly for earth, and too earthly for heaven.' Most periods in human history have been marked by a swing between these two extremes, almost like a pendulum. When believers have too great a focus on upholding the spiritual elements of our faith they forget that a holistic human is one that dwells in and is at liberty to enjoy the pleasures of this world (regulated by God, of course). This is what I refer to when I talk about spiritualism. Spiritualism is when believers have an over-emphasis on things such as righteousness, holiness, purity, etc... These are all important ideals to uphold, but spiritualism will place far more emphasis on them as foundational to the faith, at the expense of enjoyment of the beauty of the world God has created. An example is when believers held the idea that married sex was for the fulfilment of God's command in Genesis 1:28 when He said "be fruitful and multiply..." Believing that sex for a reason other than procreation is against the spiritual order of God. In fact, sex outside of this pursuit can be viewed as being equally wretched as fornication. This is very extreme, but there is another side to which the proverbial pendulum swings- the side of materialism.

Materialism is a hyper focus on the material aspects of this world; leisure, pleasure, riches, fame, possessions, all of these form part of materialistic ideals. It is no overstatement that we live in a materialistic world. We are constantly bombarded with messages that downplay our lives then offer us the solution in a bottle. We are told that we need to look prettier, drive a more comfortable car and that we deserve it all. This goes deep into our sexual lives as we are told that we deserve better, more, much more explosive sex... The focus of spiritualism is 'Pharisee-esque' in that there's an ideal of what God wants. Materialism boarders on shunning God altogether because the focus is 'me on my own terms'.

The history of the church is a long and dramatic one. Part of the drama has been the opposing forces of doctrines where some believers interpret the scriptures in isolation and thereby spawn an isolated doctrine. One such doctrine, or belief is that the Christian should concern himself only with the things of heaven, and that earth is not his/her home. This is the belief that Christians are pilgrims in this world and therefore should make no effort in enjoying its pleasures. That sounds very spiritual to me, and not the right kind of Spirit.

One Bishop Wayne Malcom once said "the Concept you have of Jesus shapes the character of your Christianity." What this means is that what you perceive Jesus Christ to be will influence how you live out your Christian faith. We see this quite prevalently in matters of financial riches. People associate [financial] poverty with piety. Somehow, this is linked to Jesus because the word says "For you know the grace of our Lord Jesus Christ, that though he was rich, yet for your sake he became poor, so that you by his poverty might become rich (2 Corinthians 8:9 ESV)." This is interpreted to mean we ought to be poor and shun riches. The story of the rich ruler also comes to mind here, along with the camel and the needle story. All these are misused to justify why Christians should shy away from earthly riches. Likewise, in sexual matters, we are conditioned to think of it as lustful and evil.

Two of the most influential characters of the New Testament are Jesus Christ and the Apostle Paul. The commonality between these two is that they were both celibate. This creates a problem, because if we are to imitate these people, we too need to be celibate. Sex becomes an obsolete notion.

However, it is the Apostle Paul himself who says he wishes that all would be celibate like him, but that each person should marry if they cannot exercise self-control (See 1 Corinthians 7:6-9). A closer look at this passage will reveal these myth-busting truths concerning this matter:

- The Apostle Paul makes it clear that what he is saying in this passage is a concession, not a command. Therefore, he is giving advice based on personal experience and preference, and not speaking with the divine authority of God.
- Each of us have our own gifts from God, in the context of the passage; marriage and celibacy are both Gifts from God. By extension, the contents of both gifts is in itself a gift (i.e. sex in marriage is a gift, children, etc. While celibacy provides the gift of exclusive service to God and His kingdom in ways other than ministering love to your spouse, children, etc...)
- Neither celibacy nor marriage is greater than the other. Both are assignments given to us by God [for the fulfilment of His divine will].

These truths have been stripped from the Christian understanding of true Christianity. Instead, we have over preached the narrative that 'sex before marriage is a sin' and it has resulted in dysfunction in many marriages. What is interesting about the notion of 'sex before marriage is a sin' is that our minds are wired to view things in 'black and white'. We perceive things in opposites; hot and cold, wet and dry, tall and short, night and day, etc. in the context of 'sex before marriage is a sin' our subconscious mind views this as 'sex before marriage is a sin' because it seeks clarity on where to place sex in our records of right/wrong, good/bad, sin/right. This is further engraved in us because of how often it is repeated and reinforced by our behaviours. This is not coincidental, because prohibitions form inhibitions.

The conundrum is that as Christians, if we fall into spiritualism, then sex will be an act of obedience rather than a service of pleasure. If we become materialistic, we fall prey to our hypersexualised culture and sex becomes a gratification of self rather than a mutual service of pleasure. So that neither of the two extremes work to make a contented and whole sexual experience that is in line with the word of God concerning married sex. Speaking of hypersexualised culture, what is it really?

Hypersexualised culture

Ever heard of the phrase *'sex sells'*? Or better, tune into any television channel, and you are likely to be met with some sexualised message... it may be an advert for perfume, alcohol, automobile, even food. It often has me wondering what sex has to do with all these products. But our culture exploits the allure of sex so much because it is effective in drawing attention and sparking a reaction (more on this in chapter 2). It's a fact that more people are likely to click on a video if the thumbnail has a 'sexy female' in revealing clothing other than a "respectable" thumbnail. It's enticing, especially for men because we're stimulated by what we see.

At the heart of sex and sexuality is our issue of our 'God-shaped vacuum'. This is an idea by Blaise Pascal which he asserts that

"What is it then that this desire and this inability proclaim to us, but that <u>there was once in man a true happiness</u> of which there now remain to him only the mark and <u>empty trace</u>, which <u>he in vain tries to fill</u> from all his surroundings, seeking from things absent the help he does not obtain in things present? But these are all inadequate, because the <u>infinite abyss can only be filled by an infinite and immutable object</u>, that is to say, only by God Himself." (Pascal, 1958)

Some people have credited the following iteration of this great truth to Pascal:

"There is a God-shaped vacuum in the heart of every person, and it can never be filled by any created thing. It can only be filled by God, made known through Jesus Christ."

However, the latter does not seem to belong to Pascal, but is a derivative of what Pascal asserted. That is, we all have an innate yearning for God and a connection with Him. Absent of this connection, we try in vain to fill it with any and all things. This is where the allure of sex comes in because sex is a gateway to deep and intimate connection, whether we admit to this or recognise it subconsciously. So when any sexual proposition is made be it an advert on TV, print media or radio, many are drawn to it for this reason-we're made to crave connection because we were created to connect. Now the enemy is aware of this and since he is anti-God, he desires to use this perversely.

This is why we have such dysfunction in society, because we are in search of a satisfaction only God can bring. Added to this, is the gender dysphoria we see in popular culture. The attack on the binary genders, along with the uprising of feminism is what has created fertile ground for sexual issues. Wives challenge the authority of their husbands and husbands retaliate in an attempt to restore their sense of authority. We are living out the curse given to Eve in the Garden of Eden... the women's desires are for their husbands. Men aren't guiltless either, because we tend to seek control from a point of entitlement and wind up abusing the leadership that we have been given by God. But there is another contributor to sex being taboo, and that is the same response we saw in Adam and Eve following the fall in Genesis; the bible says they hid from God, the question is 'why'? My conviction is that they were ashamed. Sadly, they're response to sin was not running towards the Father and seeking forgiveness, but running away and making vain attempts to course-correct only to make matters worse. This is the reality of our current state; we are still running away, even after Jesus Christ has come to reconcile us to the Father, we're running. This is the result of shame.

Shame keeps us from enjoying our sex lives

Wherever shame is, it is impossible to reach our potential in this area. If you're ashamed of who you are, you can never live out a life to the fullest potential. The shame supresses your gifts and abilities, you tread so slowly that you never take risks. It is almost as if shame breeds shame- it's debilitating. So when shame enters into the marriage bed, we never approach sex with our spouses with the appropriate mind-set to realise the gift that it is for our marriage.

Shame is the reactive feeling of guilt. Guilt because you did stuff you shouldn't have. But the interesting thing is that you had no idea how wrong these were at the time of commission. One of the words Jesus uttered on the cross in prayer was "Father, forgive them, for they know not what they do"- and I believe the same grace and forgiveness is yours for the taking this day. You no longer have to grapple with the shame and guilt of the past, just invite the Lord's spirit into your heart to bring change in that area of shame and guilt.

To understand why sex is so taboo, we'd have to look at the secular view of sex. Sex is viewed as a physical act where both parties involved use each other consensually to satisfy their needs. Sex can also involve multiple participants or even same gender or gender altered individuals... This line of thinking lands us in the realm of porn... Why is porn so popular and why do so many people struggle with it, especially men. I asked the Lord this question once and the impression I had in my heart was to look into why Satan would want to pervert sex in the first place. Satan is anti-Christ, and anti-God. So what God creates and ordains as the natural order of things, Satan perverts (I. E. Inverts, opposes, etc...) Satan's aim is to do the opposite of what God does. So sex is the only activity that has various God ordained facets... 1. It is reserved for the enjoyment of those in the institution of godly marriage. 2. Male and female were genders created by God, which makes gender God-ordained and sacred. 3. Sex in a marriage context is the righteous means by which man can partner with God in creation. Let's expand a bit on these three;

1. Sex is reserved for enjoyment in the institution of Godly marriage

This is easily opposed by the promotion of 'moving in together', open relationships, sex before marriage (which is fornication, biblically). The idea that sex should signal a sacred bond between man and wife is slowly dying, with terms such as 'body-count'[4] being normalised in society.

1. Male and female were genders created by God, which makes gender God-ordained and sacred...

I don't want to go on a lengthy discourse on this because the bible is clear about the binary nature of gender. However, this has become such an issue that we are being forced to accept that a biological male can transition into a woman, and vice-versa. We're also being propagated with the idea that gender and sex are different and that your sex is a choice. All of this is aimed at weakening the argument for marriage in the first place. As a global community, we are sliding down a very slippery slope where ills like paedophilia are likely to become legally appropriated. The idea that God, a creator of such masterful ability, would make the error of trapping a man in a woman's body is laughable. Nevertheless, He did give each of us free-will, regardless of how such will compares to His.

1. Sex in a marriage context is the righteous means by which man can partner with God in creation

Of all creation made by God, none bear his image and likeness except for mankind. After the fall, mankind was also given the responsibility of bearing the embodiment of God in Jesus Christ. This is incensing to the enemy, who not only contends with us being like God, but we're also given a saviour who is God-incarnate, and looks like us. We partner with God in creation by being conduits for bringing life to this earth. Such is the prestige that God has given us, and sex is the means. This is why you see abortion being on the rise, because the enemy of our souls is against all things pro-life.

There are others that you may find, but these three are fundamental to the enemy's strategy, which is ultimately to destabilise and abolish the nuclear family, where there is a mom and dad, in a loving marriage with children being raised in the fear of God. This is what builds strong communities, cities, and nations. Look at most of the ills out there, and they will find their purpose in the opposition of all this. LGBTQIA+, OPEN Marriages, and even feminism are all opposed to these three. In an attempt to disassociate themselves with such ills, Christians lose sight of the original intention for sex in a marriage context.

Should we get comfortable speaking about sex?

The answer to this question is not definitive. Firstly because I cannot impose anything on anyone concerning what they can or cannot speak about; this is a matter of personal choice. Secondly, there is no explicit word about this in scripture, at least not to my knowledge. Seeing that biblical scripture is what we model our faith on, it follows that we would have the bible as an authority on the matter. Some may argue that Songs of Solomon as a book is sufficient coverage on sexual matters, while other scholars would view this as an allegory of Christ and the church. Regardless of which side of the argument you fall, we can all agree that there is no definitive answer about whether or not we should get comfortable speaking about sex, at least publicly. A third reason would be born out of a question of what is meant by 'getting comfortable speaking about sex'. Some context would be helpful, but even then, we struggle in the area whether it be amongst ourselves as spouses or in larger settings as a collective of couples within a church. But to answer the question simply, I would say getting comfortable with speaking about sex would mean becoming at ease with dealing with sexual topics in a setting of Christian believers (i.e. couple's meetings) and most importantly, being able to be more articulate in our marriages as husbands and wives about sex.

I should aspire to be so comfortable with my wife that discussing sexual matters with her is no issue. As church organisations, we should also aspire to be forthcoming about sexual matters in couple's meetings so as to encourage and enrich each other's marriages. Another key element of this is finding mentors and being open to mentoring young couples on all matters, including sex. This will remove this notion of sex being taboo among Christians and help us iron out pain points before the enemy closes in on the vulnerabilities of the saints.

To put all these together, we ought to be mindful that we are not too heavenly for earth. That is, we avoid living in spiritualism, where all things are pointedly about the spiritual realm. We also need to be mindful to not give too much power to our earthly nature, thus becoming too earthly for heaven. Balance is the key, and I would invite you to keep this at the back of your mind throughout this book. Whenever you are confronted with a feeling or thought of negativity that points toward you viewing a certain element of your sexuality as taboo- ask yourself what the source is. Usually, the answer will lie at either end of the pendulum. Another element that is worth considering is your past (more on this in chapter 6). What we have been through or what we have done has a weird way of creeping into our present state, almost like a leash that limits our mobility. If you experience this, I have something to remind you; in Christ, we are new creations and the old makes way for the newness of life in Christ. Don't let the enemy cheat you of a privilege that cost Christ's innocent blood. Though the world may continue to look at you through the lens of your past, grip strongly to the newness of life in Christ.

Sex is for Pleasure in Marriage

Earlier, I made mention of an encounter I had with a group of young men attending a Christian version of a bachelor party. The party was nothing party-like, it was a gathering of men, both married and single, where we were sharing wisdom to a guy who was about to get married. There's no alcohol, girls or recreational drugs. Just words of wisdom, worship and scripture. Prior to the proceedings of this get-together, we stood outside just having a good chat with the gents, when the question of what would be our top questions for God when we get to heaven. One of the gentlemen in the circle boldly stated that his first question would be why God gave us the 'equipment' for the enjoyment of sex yet prohibits us from doing so before marriage. The conversation would continue on the difficulties of burning with passion and having to 'control your passions.'

We've all been there, guys would know this all too well. You jump out of bed and with you comes the rushing urge for sex and a huge bump down below. Some days are better than others, but this can happen several times a day and randomly without so much as a thought. Why would God design such a *fault* in us? Why couldn't He put this on pause only for it to come alive when you say I do? These were the questions being discussed in this circle and the responses were quite interesting. Here are some of mine, in answering why

God designed us to have the ability to have sex before marriage but not the permission to do so:

- We are made in the image of God, and like Him, he gave us the liberty of choice, i.e. free will. It would be against the nature of God to pre-set a function in us that would mean we only have a sexual appetite when we are married.
- It would also be incongruent with the way in which God blesses us. Often, God makes provision and equips us for our mission before the mission. So we are equipped for sex before we have the biblical right to do so, this is providence in action.
- A pre-set function that would turn on the fire of desire only when you are married would also have to turn on only when you are with your wife. Otherwise, what happens to self-control and your need to love your spouse 'and forsake all others'?
- In the spirit of self-control, a default setting of the like described above would make self-control obsolete. Why? Because you only have to control yourself if there are other forces vying for control over your 'self'. In this instance, controlling our sexual appetites not only builds our character, it also gives value to the one with whom we are married. You see, value lies in exclusivity. Think of this in anything created, when there is less of it or a limitation to its existence, it becomes more valuable. For those who have a mind for economics, when supply rises (*ceteris paribus*), price tends to dwindle so that oversupply of a 'good' lowers the price of it.

The issue of sex before marriage is one that has been widely preached in church circles. What tends to be the response in this is to think that sex is the problem. It is not, it is the condition under which it is enjoyed that the issue. Sex is inherently good, but when and how it is done determines whether or not it is good. Having sex with my wife now, after getting married, is good, doing so before we were married would not have been good. This is because I had not made a public commitment to love and to cherish her and to remain faithful to a covenant of exclusivity with her in love and the making of love, i.e. marriage.

The stigma surrounding sex and discussions of sex in the church[5] is difficult to trace, but undoubtedly plagues the married and unmarried alike. It creates no room for open and honest discussion of a topic that has become so perverted that some believe that it is unholy to engage in, even in marriage. This is part of what I aim to do in this text; to demystify sex, to speak candidly about some of the most elementary subjects relating to sex and to do so from the vantage point of the Christian mind-set. That is, to do so in a way that does not defile the reader, but calls him/her to act and improve their sex life. I am also going to be doing this with a strong emphasis on the fostering of a great relationship between spouses. This is foundational to a great sex life. I hope you enjoy the journey and that what lies in these pages empowers you to create a wonderful marriage fortified by God's grace and ever-growing pleasure in and out of the marriage bed.

Chapter 2: Sex Happens in the Mind

What is sex?

The Dictionary defines sex or sexual intercourse as "the physical activity of sex. This term is usually used to refer to sex in which a man puts his penis inside a woman's vagina" (Oxford Dictionaries, 2023). Sex also refers to touching each other's genitals. However, our expanded definition of sex now includes oral sex, anal sex and manual stimulation, which is pleasuring each other using the hands (or other objects).

It is important that we understand what is meant by sex, because the term is so taboo that we often miss what it means altogether. The main aim of sex is pleasure, yes you may argue that sex was created by God for mankind to multiply, but in that was the desire for a man and his wife to serve each other pleasure in a loving and mutually beneficial way.

Our physical interaction during sex is a manifestation of what is happening both spiritually and psychologically.[6] So this means that *sex is a mind game*. Ideally, not the kind where one manipulates the other, but a game that two participants lovingly serve each other toward blissful pleasure. All of this is possible only when the condition of the mind is right. But what is the mind?

Mind, body, spirit mind-map©

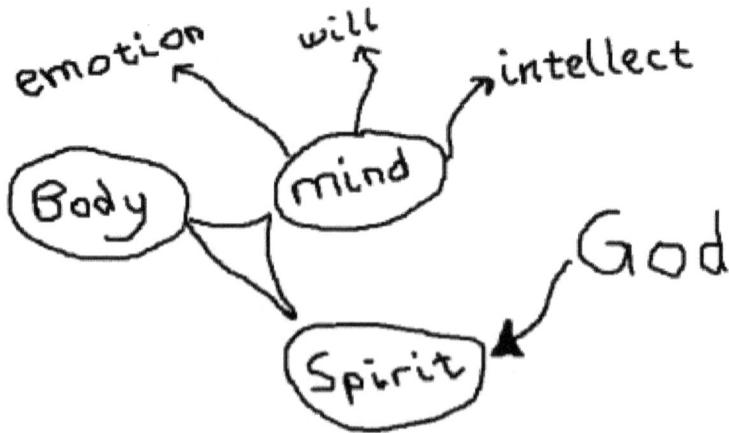

The above diagram is a recreation of a scribble I did in my diary while doing some note-taking and brainstorming on this book. The diagram depicts the elements that make-up a human being. As an aside: I used the paint app in Windows OS as it would closely resemble the diagram in my diary, so pardon my art, if it offends you ☺.

The body is a straightforward, yet complex element of the triune nature of man- what is referred to as the trichotomy of man. Give it water, food and nourishment, exercise and a regular clean, you're good to go. The complexity is in the details. But since we're not in an anatomy course in Medical Science, we'll leave the details to the physicians. What is important to remember is the need to take good care of this body as it is our licence for existing in this world. To illustrate the importance of this 'licence', Jesus needed to exist in the Flesh (i.e., the Word became flesh) for Him to be able to 'dwell among us' and fulfil the grand plan of redemption. `

This leads us to the spirit. Man's spirit is what makes man the image God, it is what distinguishes us from all other created beings. They don't have a spirit. This spirit is what merges with the Spirit of God when we accept Christ into our lives, then the process of renewal and living in righteousness begins. My elementary bible teacher used to say the Spirit of God influences our spirit, which in turn influences our mind and we see the outcome in the body. The sprit element of the trichotomy of man is a centre of consciousness, wherein we are conscious of the spiritual world. This is an area for the preacher and bible teacher, so we'll rest our analysis at this point.

The mind can be categorised into three spheres, viz. the emotions, intellect and the will.

    i. Emotions are chemical reactions that add much needed spice to life. You might hear people shunning a person who acts out of emotion, to a point where emotions are considered to be *things worth supressing*. But imagine how dull life would be without happiness? Or excitement, and a host of other positive emotions? Sure, emotions must remain under a leash, but ignoring them altogether should be crime.

This is especially true in marriage and married sex. Your spouse's emotions, as stated above, are chemical ***reactions***. This means they are a reaction to events that happen externally to their being. Ignoring these is a highway to terrible sex, or none at all. So a neat tip would be to appeal to these emotions, take care of them and avoid negative emotions. All this can be done through communication and loving understanding. Since this is a crash course, I will not delve deeper into communication nor emotion, but for our purposes, keeping your emotions and those of your spouse in check can greatly improve or sustain a hot sex life.[7]

    i. Intellect is defined as the ability to think in a logical way and understand things, especially at an advanced level (Oxford Dictionaries, 2023). In a sexual context, this means that you ought to be thoughtful, understanding and think ahead. You cannot treat your spouse unkindly all day and expect to have explosive sex in the night. You also can't expect to have sex when the other is physically ill or going through some emotional challenge like the loss of a loved one or a stressful patch at work.[8] One also has to think ahead where sex is concerned, how you may ask? Simple.

Understanding the physiological and psychological make-up of your spouse is important in understanding the concept of thinking ahead. Typically, men are quite simple in that we are driven by what we see. That is why we are so susceptible to the lust of the eyes, because imagery is usually the gateway to our stimulation. This knowledge need not be a negative in marriage, a wife who understands her husband's proneness to visual stimulation can leverage this to her own benefit. If the environment permits, she can wear much more revealing items of clothing to fire up her mate's engines. If she is comfortable with her digital security, send those nudes while he's at work and remind him of what is to come. Think ahead. For the ladies, you are much more delicate and complex. The deal, I have found with women is keeping emotional and relational harmony. If your relationship is thriving, her needs are met emotionally and relationally, then sex becomes a by-product of this. A good rule of thumb is to interrogate your wife's emotional and relational needs, a lack of sex is usually an indicator that she needs attention in these two areas.

i. The will refers to our ability to choose and act. This may seem far removed from a discussion of pleasure and married sex, but our choices are influenced by our emotions and intellect- our analysis of all facts and circumstances affecting our decision. It is wise then to tend to the emotions and intellect of both yourself and your spouse in order to positively influence the will. Proper treatment of your spouse is likely to be a better foreground for sex than any form of abuse. The principle of reaping what you sow rings true on this point. Another element of the will is action. Many of us know what we want (intellect), know how we feel (emotions) but struggle to act accordingly in addressing or responding to this knowledge. Men will feel like their sex life is waning but do nothing aside from finding another mate other than their wives who's 'more exciting.' This is a serious case of acting on misinformation. Rather than addressing your issues and understanding the root cause of the lack of sex, some people would rather go outside their marriage and create more problems for themselves.

The above *crash* course analysis of the trichotomy of man, especially of the mind gives us an idea of what we're dealing with. As is pertains to the mind, winning in the game of sex requires one to understand all of these elements of the mind, and play to their strengths while leveraging on their partner's strengths too. This way, the excitement and passion for physical intimacy never dies. All of this is born out of truly knowing your wife, which is what we'll be dealing with next.

...and Adam *knew* his wife...

The King James version of the bible uses the phrase '*knew his* wife' when it refers to sexual intercourse between spouses. An example of this is how the bible says "And Adam knew Eve his wife; and she conceived, and bare Cain, and said, I have gotten a man from the LORD (Genesis 4:1 KJV)" The word is used euphemistically to infer sex, but it is interesting that the act of intercourse would be likened to knowing someone. I believe this is because in order for us to enjoy sex we ought to know each other. So that intimate knowledge of my wife is the prerequisite for great sex.

We spend years in University and school training for a vocation, yet little to no time is spent studying and understanding our spouses. If sex is a matter of the mind, then a deep-dive into your spouse is central to a successful marriage and sex-life. This idea of knowing each other came from a podcast I was listening to by Ligonier Ministries (Presented by the late R.C. Sproul)[9] (Sproul, 2023). In this episode, the speaker advocates for intimate knowledge of your spouse by spending time together and in that time, having deep, intimate conversations. I suppose these seem very obvious for many of us, but the question is why are they so hard to implement? Most of us will admit to understanding the importance of communication and the role it plays in building up a marriage relationship. This is the 'Why' of communication in marriage. However, a large portion of married people struggle to hold meaningful conversations, which is the 'how' of communication in marriage. Writing this, I am conscious of my own deficiencies in communicating with my wife in the past and some in the present.

At the time of writing, our son was just months old. Between dealing with work, making sure he's taken care of and the rest of the responsibilities we held prior to his birth, there always seemed to be very little time left for 'deep, meaningful conversation'. We'd be in a situation where I'd get to bed and my wife had fallen asleep, or I am too exhausted to be chatty, often dosing-off midway through our chat.

Contrast this to how well we communicated prior to getting married- the difference is amazing. When we lived apart, we'd have what we called "T-time"[10], an hour dedicated to catching up, **daily**. Not to mention the countless 'how's your day going" texts we'd send throughout the day. I always felt like I knew every little detail of my wife's life during those times, even when we were physically apart. A mere break of 2-3 hours unannounced would be met with grumpy tantrums because I had broken the connection. I'll admit that our communication now is not quite what it was, but there are a number of lessons we can learn on how to create an ongoing culture of healthy communication from the days of old.

1. Make time for communication.

    As mentioned above, we had T-time. This refers to Thabethe-Time, an hour that often turned into two or three hours of non-stop, back-and-forth conversation, either via text or call. Our friends, the Thwala's, called it their *conference call*. I remember that he (my friend) would always be unavailable at 9pm for a call with his now wife. Those were the days ☺ . What made these arrangements a success, is that we prioritised time to connect.

I am aware that life can get in the way, and that you have far greater opportunity when you live together, but that does not eliminate the need and benefit for a planned moment of connection. The idea of planning out time may be uninteresting for some because it lacks the spontaneity that is often associated with romance. I have a different perspective; when you make time for conversation, it declutters your mind and schedule, making you less likely to go for long without having time to connect as a couple. What it also does is it eliminates the guilt that you may feel when you read passages like this while knowing that you lack in the area of your version of *T-time*. Instead, you're comforted by the time you have planned for connection.

Lastly, planning this time out usually makes you much more intentional during the time, often bringing forth feelings and experiences you have accumulated for sharing with your beloved spouse. In the end, planning anything ahead doesn't make it less special, it's actually that much more special because you intentionally make time for it.

1. Prioritise getting inside your spouse's mind

By this I mean that you should be concerned about what your significant other felt about their experiences. We often dwell so much on chatting about what person 'X' did and we forget to hone in on how the person telling the story felt, why they felt that way and chiefly, how they would want us (the listener) to react to this. Women are typically great at covering both aspect. They tell a story with so much animation and willingly express how they felt in the situation without having to be coerced. Men on the other hand tend to have difficulty juggling both, it is usually one or the other; either he will tell a story and not express the emotion or he will physically express the emotion without the story, rarely ever verbalising how it makes him feel. The key in all this is to explore the internal state of affairs, not what happened outwardly.

For an example, if my wife tells me that her colleague spoke rudely to her, my aim should not be to take her side and say 'XYZ has always been rude to you, she should find a cliff and jump off"... rather, my aim should be to extract relevant information from this story, i.e. why do you think what your colleague said is rude? Why are you so hurt about it or how do you feel about it? Would you like to know my thoughts on the matter? ... This may sound rehearsed and calculated, but it is such questions that we fail to ask. What ends up happening is that the spouse telling the story feels like they have shared their feelings and experience in the situation, when in truth, they're just telling you what happened and not how they experienced it. The listening spouse is likely to walk away having misconceptions about how their spouse felt and that they did well listening, when in fact they did not. The point is that you need to be an active listener, and active listening involves asking probing questions.

1. You have to talk to your spouse, about everything

Back to our *T-time* moments of old. I used to be so excited by the fact that I would later have a chance to speak to my lover about the most incidental details of my day. In fact, the excitement was so great that I often told her about what I was keeping for *T-time* during the day. By the time we had our *T-time*, I would either repeat my story, now going into the details or tell her about something entirely different. Regardless of what happened eventually, we'd go way past the hour mark because there was just so much to cover. To put you at ease, none of it was ever boring.

1. Give the gifts that the spouse wants, not what you want.

I suppose this segment is less about what the gift is and more about the gift itself. I always think that giving good gifts to your spouse is a result of good listening. Most people are very forthcoming about what they want in life when you are in intimate relationship with them. My wife, for example, will often say what she wishes for in passing conversation. To the untrained ear, this would be a passing comment brushed aside as 'one of those things'. But to a discerning ear, this is a hint of what it is she wishes for. Ahead of the first Mother's day after our son's birth, she'd been raving about this bottle of perfume. Raving is a bit overstated, but I believe she only mentioned it one or two times. I caught onto this and got her a bottle for a gift. To say she was surprised doesn't do her reaction any justice, I scored so many points by doing this I regretted not doing it as often. What made the gift a success is not the gift, it's listening and having an intimate relationship.

There are two parts to this gift giving, the first is having an intimate relationship. The second is listening with a discerning ear. A discerning ear will help you determine 'how badly' your spouse wants a thing. The intimacy will create an environment where your spouse will be forthcoming about their want, desires and aspirations in life. In the perfume example above, there were other things she said she wanted. Some of which I could not even afford at the time, but she wanted them either way. Mine was to fish out what mattered more to her and what I could afford.

As for giving of gifts itself, this is a great way of tokenising your love for each other. Love is intangible, but the physical nature of gifts is an embodiment of this love. While I admit that some gifts may be intangible, physical gifts stand as long-lasting tokens upon-which memories can be imputed. Take wedding rings for example; they are symbols of love and each couple has a unique story about their wedding rings. Yet the presence or absence of a ring does nothing to the existence of love and relationship between a married people. For example, my uncle had been married over 35 years at the time of his passing. He never wore a wedding ring, partly because he worked with metals and it was impractical for him to wear jewellery on his hands. I on the other hand wear my wedding band all the time. Does it mean my marriage is more real than my uncle's? Not one bit, it is a matter of preference, but the ring I wear is a sure reminder and public symbol of the fact that I am married.

1. Zoom into intimacy- the nightly questionnaire

I was listening to the many things I listen to one day and the person speaking was talking about the importance of having a 'full day'. What he described as a full day is one where you experience one of these three at least once each day; laughter, crying, and deep thought. The laughter is a no-brainer, the benefits of laughing are so well documented. It improves health, and exercises facial muscles. The crying was a bit of a shocker for me, until I learnt that men are capable of crying out of joy (other men, not me, lol). The idea of crying speaks to the depth of emotion that elicits the tears. This is not to say squeeze your eyes out for a full day. But tapping into deep emotion at least once a day is important. Then lastly, the idea of deep thought. The distinction of 'deep' thought is a means of differentiating this from the endless thoughts you have as you go through each day. Deep thought is intentional, enriching and often life-changing. I find that I experience this when I read or listen to educational sermons or podcasts. Anything that causes you to ponder with intention is good here. So the questions to ask in summary:

1. What made you laugh?
2. What made you cry?
3. What made you think?

These questions are better than 'how was your day' because the response you get is usually the same as the one you get when you greet people and ask them how they are doing- *good*. Intimate conversation is like peeling through the layers that we often put on in order to function in the world. It cuts through all the facades and masks we put on to pretend that everything is okay. We get to the inner thoughts, the fears, anxiety and hopes of each other. It is here where we are able to offer measured and intentional support, but also earn the due trust that we are capable of treating the intimate intellectual property of our spouse with grace and respect, not publicising it for all the world to see. This leads me to the next point, *compassion and empathy*.

1. Compassion and Empathy

We're made in the image of one God, but we are so different from each other. What breaks my heart could be a non-issue for my wife. This is where empathy comes through. When your spouse shares intimate details about themselves or how they are feeling, this is an opportunity for you to show empathy by looking at their story from the lens of their personality and experience, not yours. Our view of the world is largely influenced by our personality and experiences, this is how we tend to interpret the happenings in and around our lives. By personality, I refer to your inclinations, passions, preferences, etc... While experiences points to our past, what we have been through, our knowledge base and so on. Empathy is the ability to disregard our own personality and experience when evaluating what we're hearing, by getting into the shoes of the *storyteller.*

The compassion then, is in how you respond to what you hear. Jumping to explain about your day without taking time to ask follow-up questions or even enquire about the role you can play to show support is the ultimate antithesis to compassion. Compassion goes deeper to a state of being with your spouse in the pain they feel. Though you may not necessarily feel the pain as much as they feel it, but seeing them in pain is what pains you. The story may not be a painful one, it may be joy. Regardless of the emotion or feeling, you feel the same way because you love your spouse and what bring them joy makes you joyous too.

1. Retuning the question is not returning the favour

Wife: How was your day?

Husband: It was good. How was yours?

Stranger 1: Hello, how are you?

Stranger 2: I am good. How are you?

This is snip of the common dialogue between people in varying degrees of relationships and closeness. They're fundamentally the same. The one person asks how the other's day is, and the responder says 'good' and hastens to return the question. Somehow this registers as politeness in our minds. Sadly, in marriage, this doesn't always mean polite; it screams 'disengaged'. Sure, you may be excited to hear about your spouse's day right after he/she tells you how it went. But take time to let that sink in and ask further clarity-seeking questions per the guidelines above. The idea is that you don't make conversation between you (couple) be about you (individual) but make the conversation about you (couple). If you want to test this theory, the next time you greet someone with whom you're not in a very close relationship with and they ask you how you're doing, just tell them "I'm not good" and see the level of interest they have in your not being good. I tried this at work, and the response was a cold disinterest followed by moving onto the issue at hand, which was work, work and more work.

Looking back at what our communication was like prior to getting married, it's a wonder that our bond was as good as it was despite us not engaging in sex. Frankly, that is the foundation upon which our marriage is built today. The reason for this is that the quality of the relationship you have with your spouse is directly correlated to the quality of your conversations. Sex then is a by-product of that relationship, and quality sex cannot happen outside of a quality relationship.

Marriage is not about sex and I believe that wholeheartedly. I also believe that marriage cannot exist without a decent amount of healthy sex. What that means is that sex is not marriage but marriage is hardly marriage without it. Ask any couple who are going through a rough time in their marriage, or one that has had trouble in the past. 99.99% of the time, no sex is taking place during the rough patches. This is because our sex lives mirror where we are relationally. Another proof of this is how biologically, there have been natural barriers to sex that have been uniquely placed by God in our lives, i.e. Periods, Child birth and even sickness. In these times, though there would be no fights between a couple, sex is just not a thing. These are the times where ministering love to each other becomes about something more than your physical interaction.

Now you see me

To be seen is one of, if not mankind's biggest craving. We want attention. We want to be noticed, I believe that this somehow validates our existence. Giving this to your spouse throughout the day is a better strategy than not doing so and expecting sex at the end of the line. Men are usual culprits here, we often see changes we don't acknowledge. A woman will spend two hours (or even more) at the salon pursuing that perfect hairstyle, only to come home to *Mr. Grumpy* who doesn't even notice the change. Word of advice, the next time your wife comes home look out for any changes, screen her for something that is worthy of acknowledgement. Anything new on her should be appreciated. Appreciate the time it took for her to put it together, because most times it is done with your praise in mind. The same goes for the ladies; if your husband does something good for you, appreciate him. He didn't have to, and you're not deserving of it- it is by the Grace of God that you have a husband willing to do good by you. Appreciate God and appreciate him for being an instrument of God's ministry of love in your life. Notice that in my presented examples the wife/woman seems to crave being seen for how she looks and the husband seeks acknowledgement for what he does. This is not a mistake, because men generally want to be respected for their actions more than women. In our household, I take pride in the fact that I am a great provider, protector and teacher. My wife on the other hand, tends towards being a nurturer and is more concerned about how things look, including herself. Not out of being vain, but it seems to matter to her more than it does to me. It's how many of my married friends and people I have encountered are, and every married person needs to 'see' their spouse.

Seeing each other is a matter of consciousness. Telling your spouse how you appreciate what you're seeing is a matter of confidence. When I see the beauty of my wife, it is simply a fact that I am conscious of. It is great that I am aware of it, but it is useless to her if I do not vocalise it. Telling her that I think she looks beautiful, repeatedly, will boost her confidence and usually results in her having more enthusiasm for doing things that accentuate that beauty, i.e. hairstyles, fashion, etc... So get in the habit of complimenting each other, appreciating the things that the other does for you. Breathe psalms and hymns in your house, adopt the attitude of Gratitude and sex will happen almost organically. You see, people think sex is only physical, it is not, sex is the culmination of physical, spiritual and soul forces and nothing speaks to all three as well as an attitude of gratitude.

To draw from the trichotomy of man as analysed above, we see that we are a three-part being. Through our body, we are 'world conscious'. We have senses through which we detect and interact with the happenings of our surroundings. With our spirit, we are God-conscious. We are 'aware' of the things of God and the happenings in the spirit realm. This is why the most hurtful experiences (like losing a loved one) affect us so much, because our spiritual reality is much more powerful than the physical reality. Lastly, with our soul/mind we are self-conscious. It is how we are conscious of what is going on inside, so that the mind is really the connection between the spirit and the flesh. This all sounds theological, or even mythical. The point of it all is to illustrate how appealing to your spouse's mind has a far reaching effect than you simply 'getting lucky'. It cultivates a healthier sense of self, brings clarity to the reality of the love of God and manifests itself in an outlook of confidence which is often seen in what people call 'the glow'.

Why sex sells?

Craving for connection- Genesis 1:26

Man was created by God in His image, after His own likeness. Most times people get caught up in the trends of body positivity and assume that our physical appearance is the image of God that the scriptures refer to. They assume that God is this multi-faceted being who is fat, thin, tall and short. After all, your outward appearance is a consequences of habit; you are what you eat mashed up with your level of activity and genetics. This is not the '*you*' being referred to in Genesis 1:26.

When the scripture refers to man being created in the image of God, it refers to the inner person being reflective of God. We see this in Jeremiah, when God says before he formed him in his mother's womb, He knew him. The Jeremiah God knew prior to formation is not the physical Jeremiah, but the Spirit-Jeremiah whom was ordained a prophet before birth. Now all this shows us that we are like God in matters concerning our inner man. Chief among our characteristics is our need for connection.

Connection is how we relate to the things and people around us. In fact, we were created to connect with other humans. This is why God does not desire for us to be worried about what we will eat, wear and other needs of the flesh. We ought not to serve money (Mormon) because we were not created to chase after *things* but *things* were designed to aid us in our human experience and connecting with others. Connection with others is therefore the chief desire of our inner man; this is what makes us like God. God desired to connect with man from the beginning of man's existence. When man broke this connection by falling into sin, God pursued a plan to re-connect to man so much that He gave His son to mediate between a fallen man and

Himself. So that by His son, Man could be reconnected to God. This is why religion is so dangerous, because it places emphasis on doing stuff rather than accepting an invitation to relationship and connection with God through Jesus Christs, so how does sex come into the picture here? Easily... Sex is a means for connection... I submit to you that the true allure of sex is the connection, not the physical pleasure. This is why having sex with multiple partners never satisfies, because there is no connection. Yet having multiple sexual encounters with one partner deepens the connection. Here lies the power of sex and its allure for those in the marketing space; it is an invitation to connection via an innate appetite that we all have.

Our culture exploits the allure of sex so much because it is effective in drawing attention and sparking a reaction (chapter 1). Sex and all things sexual are attractive, because at a sub-conscious level, they communicate a call to connection, which is what all humans crave. We ought to remember that the creation of Eve was a response to man's need for connection. Prior to the moment God decides to create Eve for Adam, he had not said anything was 'not good'. The first time we have record of God uttering the words 'It is not good' is in response to man's lack of connection.

Designing Your Sex Life Vision?

We're rarely advised to design a vision for our lives, at least not specifically. We hear about goals for the year when phrases like "new year, new me" are thrown around in conversation. Goals, to-dos and dreams are all bits that make up what we want our lives to turn out to be. So why not design a vision for your life and let the goals and to-dos be guided by the ultimate vision. This is the idea in building your sex life vision. How often do you want to have sex, how do you want it? Where do you want it? All these and other questions are worth discussing with your spouse and considering in your own space. Designing a vision for your sex life does a couple of things for you.

i.   It causes you to become conscious of what you want. If you know what you want, you're likely to find out why you want it. I realise that our generation is good at knowing what they want but not at why they want it. We are so out of tune with our inner selves because we have been so misinformed, mis-educated and misdirected. We hate on people because some bi influencer 'cancelled' them, without interrogating the reasons why. We need to be more conscious of ourselves and what we are thinking.

i. It makes you intentional about change and being consistent in the things that make your vision a reality. You see, knowing what you want to become can guide you in charting a plan on how you are going to achieve this. For example, if we want to run a marathon, we are likely to do the things that will aid us in succeeding in this vision. These will include exercise, diet and sleep habits. It may not include running the marathon the next morning, but small incremental steps towards the ultimate goal. Likewise, you won't begin having sex daily the way you want it and how you want it the day after deciding to pursue your sex life vision. It's small, measured and intentional steps that will get you there over time.

i. It keeps you from stumbling. What often helps us in avoiding the things we do not want is clarifying what we actually want. I work hard because I hate being poor. So because I know what I want, I am better able to identify things that do not align with this, i.e. what I don't want. It's the great power of opposites. In my sex life, I want to remain faithful to my wife and to preserve the purity of our marriage. Just like God, I hate divorce, and I would not want my sexuality and sex to be used by the enemy as a weapon to destroy my marriage. Hence my drive in equipping myself with knowledge and understanding in this area so that I can fortify my marriage in it.

i. You feel a sense of accomplishment. What you cannot measure you cannot control. If I say I want to lose weight, I need to know what my current weight is, and what the target weight is. But even more so, I need to understand the concept of weight and have a means of quantifying it...i.e. Kilograms, pounds, etc... this all seems basic because we have a concept of the relative nature of body mass, i.e. weight. The more weight I lose, the closer I move toward my target weight and the better I feel about my progress. The same goes for our sex lives, it may be weird to track the number of times you are having sex in a month, but I would be more concerned with improving my sex life than with the weirdness of counting the number of times I am having sex with my wife.

During my days as a student in University, we learnt about a concept called S.M.A.R.T.[11] what this acronym stood for was **S**pecific, **M**easurable, **A**ttainable, **R**elevant and **T**ime-bound. This was a model used to evaluate the soundness of any strategic goal. If it failed to meet any of the criteria per this acronym, it was a deficient goal. In designing your Sex Life Vision®, consider the following:

- Is your vision **specific**? '*I want to have more sex*' is not the same as '*I want to have sex with my husband/wife a minimum of 5 times a week except for a hiatus during periods or other unavoidable stoppage*'. The first statement is open-ended, the latter details what you want, how many times you want it and the various situations where exceptions can be made. It can be further enhanced by specifying how long you want to last, the kind of sexual positions you want to explore, etc... the key thing is for it to have specifics and for it to be tailored to your desires.
- Is your vision **measurable**? In other words, do you have the means to document, track and account for the progress that you make towards achieving your vision? Again, tracking your sex life might sound absurd to the immature mind. What you don't realise is that people who feel dissatisfied with anything are likely to understate their progress and overstate their failures, i.e. if you feel you are fat, you are likely to overstate the severity of this observation and minimise any positives toward changing it. So keeping track allows you to face the facts honestly and analyse your progress objectively. Trust me, I do assurance work for a living, I live for identifying negatives and finding positives in anything is always mental gymnastics for me. Another aspect of measurability is the concept

of understanding what success looks like for *you*. We all want a great sex life, but this means different things for different couples. Find out what it is for you and your spouse, this way, you are pulling in the same direction.

- Is your vision **attainable**? This is a relative question, but there are cases where it can be an evaluation of absolutes. For instance, the moral understanding of a Christian does not permit partaking in an orgy. So it is unattainable for a Christian to partake in an orgy of have this as part of their Sex Life Vision®. On the other hand, making-out at a movie theatre and finishing off with steamy sex at home or in the car is another thing entirely. Although this is a fantasy, it may be part of your overall vision to become more adventurous in sex and this example could be one of the manifestations of this. Your ability to attain your vision should therefore align with your values and the practicality of whatever vision you have.

- Is your vision relevant? I don't think that anyone, by any stretch of the imagination, would ever partake in something that is irrelevant to them. Likewise, it would be imprudent to design a vision that is not relevant to you. Just like the orgy example above, it is not relevant to a Christian whose values conflict with the act of orgies.

- Is your vision **time-bound**? Our time on earth is limited, so we ought to do all we can with this understanding in mind. It would be unwise for me to say my vision is to have sex daily or however many times without specifying 'by when' I would want to see this taking place. Placing time-frames to visions and goals incentivises us to "redeem the time" and to take appropriate action in the appropriate season. Imagine this in the context of bearing children; if you and your spouse wanted to have children but never specify when you want to pursue this vision, you may get to your seventies and realise that you are both childless and physically incapable of bearing children at that age[12]. This is why I am a firm advocate for taking appropriate action, in the appropriate manner and the appropriate season.

Knowing the locus of sex and the various elements to it is key to success in this area. Having dealt with the mind, the next chapter deals with the body. It is a biological fact that we engage sexually using our physical bodies, understanding this aspect of the sexual experience is beneficial to the person who wants a great sex life. An important component of this is the positions we take during (and after sex) and their differences. In our next chapter we will tackle the subject of sex positions; what they are, why they are and how they are performed. Enjoy!

Chapter 3: Sex Positions

Sex is an act we partake in using our bodies. It goes without saying that these need to be kept in working order to fulfil the duties we have to each other as spouses. By duties, I am referring to each spouse's responsibility to serve the other sexually. What is evident when you speak to Christians about sex is that they usually have a go-to position and they believe that's it. Now this is not wrong, and do not take what I am about to discuss to be an indictment of having a go-to position. Rather, my aim is to expose you to the various positions you can try to add some variety to your sexual repertoire and keep the flames of passionate attraction and intimacy burning ever so hot. In the discussion of sex, and specifically sex position, we tend to forget the position we ought to take after sex. In fact, it is not even considered a position at all. In this chapter we'll be dealing with all things sex positions during and after sex.

It's how you do it

Sex positions are one of the hottest talking points in the area of sex. If you don't believe me, read into the history of the missionary position. People from generation to generation have grappled with the ideal form during sex. Questions such as "is it godly for a woman to be on top of a man?" how does the bible prescribe sex to be had? Saints, sex positions are nothing more than a formation in sports. In football (or soccer, for American readers), you have 11 players on the field, regardless of the formation. Any of these players can score goals, defend, attack, etc... participation in the game does not require any special player except for the handling of the ball (which is reserved for the goalkeeper only). The analogy of sex positions as a formation in sports is particularly intriguing, because the formation is set according to the game-plan or strategy you have going into sex. Strategy and game-plan might sound misplaced in a sexual context but imagine getting your spouse fired up for sex and not having a clue how to sustain that momentum? This is where sex positions are important. Knowing how to pull them off becomes important by extension and having a couple of them to choose from is an added bonus.

Sex positions- why they're important

- Longevity

Lasting long in bed is a well-documented topic. Not because so many people are getting a hang on it, but it is the proverbial *holy grail* of sexual prowess. Most adverts about sex or sexual products are about pleasure, self-interest, and insecurity. The insecurity lies in the fact that men would want bigger genitals and 'lasting longer', whereas women want more fluid, tighter vaginas, bigger breasts and buttocks, or last longer. Self-interest is wrapped around 'becoming a better lover' enjoying a better sex life, all of which are presented from the position of 'self'... and pleasure is always a guarantee, we all want pleasure in life. But longevity is the one sell that promises all of these because lasting longer means a boost for one's ego, extension of pleasure and a cover for insecurity. So the longevity is how long you can sustain a sexual act/position based on your fitness. Simply, it's how long can it be done before discomfort or climax.

- Connection

This is often a key concern for the women. Connection refers to the closeness during sex. For example, a husband entering his wife from behind while she's on 'all-fours' (doggy) would be rated as being less connected than a spooning position, or even missionary. Why? Because the latter examples encompass an element of cuddles and being close together. Spooning might subconsciously communicate safety as the husband wraps his arms around the wife. For our purposes, this is what I mean by connection.

- Depth, size and stimulation a.k.a DSS (anatomical matters)

The angle at which a man 'enters' determines the point of stimulation, and depending on his size, the depth and intensity of this stimulation. Size, like lasting longer, is an issue of great discussion amongst men. The fact is, not all penises are created equal. Having said this, all men need to play to their strengths. Another element that is less spoken about is that a penis typically goes into a vagina, and they too aren't created equal. Some women are short and tight, while others are tall and wide. I have a conviction about this, in fact two. First, women who compare penises are typically experienced in sex- and it's usually not in a good way. Second, if you stick to one partner, your vagina somehow shapes up to their size and build to accommodate them thus making sex enjoyable as you stick to one partner. This, I believe, is the secret to great sex in a faithful marriage.

Sex positions - a myriad of options

Let me be clear from the start, I will not cover too many positions in this book. This is because there are so many positions out there, it would be necessary to have a separate book going through each one. In fact there are a few in antiquity like the *Ananga Ranga*, *Kuma Sutra* and many more I am sure[13]. My objective here is to present you with a few to get you started. But more than just giving you sex positions, I will rate each one in the categories of longevity, closeness and DSS.

- **Missionary Position**

This is probably the most widely known position of all. I would encourage you reading up on why it is called the missionary position, but the term somehow finds itself in church history. There are theories that the church believed that semen flowed with gravity, and so having the woman under the man would lead to conception (Priest, 2001). A closer look of this idea will indicate how sex was perceived to be chiefly concerned with procreation and not recreation. The idea of this position is that the man is atop the woman, typically with his legs in-between hers and penetrating her vagina with his penis. The in-and-out stroking is usually the responsibility of the man on this one, but this does not preclude the woman from moving. In fact, when both husband and wife move, it enhances the pleasure.

I hope this does not ruin your view of roast chicken, but in our house, when we talk about missionary-position sex with a motionless wife we refer to her as being a spring/roast chicken. Some women miss out on an enhanced experience by not playing an active role in sex by just laying down like a corpse and having the husband do all the work. Try moving a little, gyrating your hips a bit and see if it does nothing for your pleasure and that of your husbands.

A tip for the women on this one is to engage your pelvic floor muscles. This can be done by practicing what is called Kegel exercises. You can find tutorials on these online, but they are basically the musculature you use to control the flow of urine. Mastering control of these can help women tighten and loosen things down there at their will, which will increase pleasure for husbands. Doing the same is also advisable for the guys, as it improves control over your ejaculation.

A tip for the guys on the missionary position, quit racing to ejaculation. Savour the moment. Alternate between fast and slow strokes. Hard and soft also does it. Or mix all four, i.e. hard and soft thrusts coupled with fast and slow strokes[14]. You can also increase these gradually as you wish, moving from slower strokes with soft thrusts to harder thrusts with faster strokes. The idea is to spice things up, keeping your wife guessing. Avoid making use of counting methods where you do 4 soft and 1 hard, or other variations of this. I find that this distracts you from enjoying the moment, and it is detectible by your wife, making the experience more mechanical. I also appeal to wives to allow themselves to enjoy the experience of these hard-soft and slow-fast variations, sometimes you may feel like you're nearing the edge and your husband suddenly slows down. This is not a restart of your orgasm, it is 'delayed-gratification' at its best. Exercise patience and enjoy each moment for what it is.

A final word on missionary is that it is quite intensive on your back, so I'd advise men to prioritise leg-day: squats, calf-raises, and definitely deadlifts for hamstrings and your lower back. You generate power from these areas and strengthening them can only do you good. Core strength is also a plus, so your planks and leg-raises are ideal for this. Cardio workouts will help you avoid being out of breath in the intense moments of sex, so both spouses need to get active. I also found that my arms do a lot to prop up my upper body, so I basically need strength overall. Women can consider laying a pillow or another soft object under their bum to elevate themselves during missionary-position sex. This alters the angle of entry and increases the likelihood of penile stimulation of the G-spot, which is a pleasure spot within your vagina around your pubic region, it feels spongy to the finger and is very sensitive to stimulation. The husband can use his fingers to manually stimulate this spot at the intensity and direction of the wife during foreplay.

Missionary position will be the only 'man-on-top' position I will be other than *Edge of the Bed*. There are others out there, but the idea is the same: man is on top and controls most of the movement.

Ratings: Longevity 8.5/10, Closeness 10/10, DSS 7/10... The longevity depends on fitness and your ability to last. It doesn't make a 10/10 because it is not one you can do for a very long time because it also adds at least two-thirds of the husband's weight on his wife. So depending on your body mass, this may not be such a long ride. In terms of closeness, this is as good as it gets. You are face-to-face with each other and belly-to-belly. The wife can access most of the significant parts of her husband with her hands, stroking his arms and touching his back, pulling him close to her breasts and even kissing on the mouth. DSS also gets a high rating because in this position, there are ways of maximising on depth of reach and intensity of stimulation, i.e. the pillow tip above, which make missionary position more enjoyable.

- **Woman-on-top positions**

I will come right out and say it- this is most men's favourite position. Don't ask how I know this, but trust me. If you are a lady, ask your husband how he feels when you initiate sex and take charge by being on top. You can email me his response and your thoughts, but I am pretty confident that this is met with great appreciation.

The beauty of this position of sex is that there is eye contact, and the husband can feast his eyes on the face, breast and even the genital area of his wife. If you are as adventurous as to invert this position so that the wife's back faces the husband (i.e. back-to-face), it gives him the view of her buttocks. All these angles and sights are coupled with the ability to touch and feely. Now, in sex, this is a good thing because the husband can stimulate areas of his wife's body that are highly sensitive to touch and cause her arousal to spike, i.e. her nipple area or her bottom (if she's coming in reverse). The most crucial of access that a husband has to his wife in the face-to-face version of girl-on-top position, the husband has visual of his bride's clitoris. This is the most pleasure sensitive part. It is a bean-shaped figure that protrudes above the vaginal opening. Stroking this area while she is on top also increases pleasure. If the husband is blessed with arms that are long enough, and he elevates his back to about 45 degrees or more, almost touching the wife's back with his chest, he can have access to her clitoris from behind. In fact, try accessing it this way while you are both dressed and see what the reaction will be. While you are at it, take care that you give the neck some attention with your mouth and tongue.

The point is that these positions present such a great opportunity for the wife to 'mount' her husband and control the speed of strokes and intensity of her landing. It is good to mention at this point the pay-off from doing pelvic floor exercises; women with strong musculature in this area have the ability to tighten-and-loosen their 'grip' to enhance pleasure. They can alternate between intensity, speed and force of landing. You need to be fit for this one.

In this face-to-face version of girl-on-top positions, she also has access to his chest area, leaning onto him and caressing him as she pleases. But he too can play an active role in enhancing her fun. By moving your buttocks up-and-down, to meet her landing on your pelvis, you can enhance the fun.

Ratings: Longevity 8.5/10, Closeness 8/10, DSS 7.5/10... Similar to the missionary positon, the longevity on this one depends on fitness and your ability to last. In these positions, the wife's entire body can be atop her husband. Some people like this, but it is not easy to sustain for long. Woman-on-top positions are up there in terms of closeness, not quite like missionary, but this depends on your personal taste and variation. I give it a high-enough rating because it is possible to make eye-contact during sex in some variations of this position. DSS is slightly higher than missionary, because the full range of the male penis is inside his wife, and the wife has greater control over the angle in which she feels most stimulated. All the husband needs to do is to stay hard, and enjoy. However, it may be harder for some women to climax from this position because it may not be as deep, and the whole act is more physically engaging.

- **Rear-entry (a.k.a doggy style)**

The downside on this one is that there is no eye contact. For the guys, the wife from this angle is typically a sight to see. I have no idea why, but there is something about a man seeing his wife's backside. However, the other discomfort is with the association of this position with how dogs copulate. My take is that it is simply an issue of mechanics, so if it is something you feel comfortable with, it shouldn't be an issue.

Rear-entry is quite deep, in terms of entry, it is also very intense because of the nature of the position. Since the wife is either kneeling, or laying down, the buttocks and muscles around are being used to hold her up. In some case, she can even tighten her legs, making the intensity even greater. You may have read that this is the position for couples trying to get pregnant, it is not without cause that such a claim is made. Done right, rear entry positions are very deep. Another thing to note is that I am referring to rear-entry in the sense that the husband penetrates his wife's vagina from behind. This is not to be associated with anal sex, which was my assumption and the cause of my reluctance to try this position.

Ratings: Longevity 9.5/10, Closeness 5/10, DSS 9/10... I will simplify the justification for my rating thus: high DSS, low closeness and high longevity. I took half a point from longevity on account of the strain on the back and knees, depending on the surface on which you perform the position. You can also enjoy this one for long because the husband doesn't put much of his body weight on his wife, unless she lays flat. The DSS, I will leave to imagination and you trying it. Closeness is a 5 because it is neither here nor there, it is actually a trade-off between eye-contact and the sight of the wife's backside for the husband.

- **Spooning**

For the women blessed with a larger frame, this can be difficult to pull off. Spooning involves laying on your side, with the wife's back against her husband's chest- like spoons bundled together. From this position, the husband can make entry by his penis into the vagina from behind. This is a rather sensual position, as the hands are free to engage in a range of touching and caressing. Combining this position with some of the tips given above about making use of your hands would serve you well. Do not neglect making use of your lips and tongue, especially in the neck area, which is a sensitive erogenous zone for most.

Depending on the man's size plus the frame of both him and his wife, this is not a very deep sex position, i.e. the entry isn't all that deep. Some women can derive pleasure from this position, but it is unlikely to stimulate the G-spot or A-spot, which are further into the vagina. The allure of this position is the closeness of the infamous butt area, which is a stimulant for most men.

The challenge with this position is the range of motion is limited. Since you are pivoting on your hip area, moving it can be a challenge so that making an in-and-out motion with your genitals is a mission.

Ratings: Longevity 6.5/10, Closeness 8.5/10, DSS 4.5/10... These are obviously subjective, and I am not at liberty to say whether or not they are from experience... but the longevity is decent given that the stimulation is usually minimal in this position. The closeness is quite high given the skin to skin contact, but the downside is that you are not face-to-face. DSS gets a low rating, in fact it could be lower, but the factors that go into it are different from couple to couple.

- **Edge of the bed**

This position is when the wife lays on her back, with her bottom on the **edge of the bed** (or other suitable surface). She elevates her legs so that they lean against her husband's chest, having her upper body perpendicular to his. He stands on the edge to allow his penis access to her vagina.

This is a position that requires a basic level of fitness, especially the wife's core, because she has her feet up in the air throughout the sex session. The beauty of this one is that you are face-to-face, and the husband has access to his bride with his hands and the full range of his penis. With the wife's legs wide open, he can penetrate really deeply. Caution is required on the surface on which the husband stands; stable and non-slippery does the trick. Here too, the clitoral stimulation while penetrating doubles the pleasure. Similar to missionary, you can alternate the speed of your strokes and the force of your thrusts.

Ratings: Longevity 9.5/10, Closeness 10/10, DSS 10/10... Here too, like missionary, the longevity depends on fitness and your ability to last. It makes a 10/10 because it is one you can do for a very long time because it adds none of the husband's weight on his wife. So your body mass is irrelevant. However, suspending the legs in the air or spreading them for long may require a basic level of fitness for the wife. In terms of closeness, like missionary, this is as good as it gets. You are face-to-face with each other and free to touch at will. The wife can access most of the significant parts of her husband with her hands, stroking his arms and touching his back, pulling him close to her breasts and even kissing on the mouth, which will morph into missionary. DSS also gets a high rating because in this position, the angle of entry maximises on depth of reach and intensity of stimulation. You can use a pillow if needed, but this doesn't require any props. Further, if you are not tall enough, consider a new bed or surface, or you can make use of an aerobic step... Get creative and enjoy your best sex life now.

- **Straddle on a seat**

I got this from a couple with whom we are friends. The husband enthrones himself on a seat of your choosing. Preferably one that is comfortable and not too high. Then the wife straddles him like she's riding a motorbike. The genitalia meet, and the explosion of pleasure ensues.

This is a position that favours women with a decent height, although some alterations can be made to compensate for a challenge in this area. Most of the movement is the wife's and she is in charge of everything similar to the girl-on-top positions. Depending on your height, you could be doing this face-to-face and able to access each other using your hands, and mouths.

Ratings: Longevity 7/10, Closeness 10/10, DSS 8/10... the longevity here, like everywhere else depends on fitness and your ability to last before orgasm. But with practice, this should see drastic improvement as you learn to control your ejaculation (men) and know when you are about to cross that line. The downside is the level of comfort that is taken away by the chair, and the fact that the wife's entire weight is on the husbands lap. This may not be an issue for the husband, but suspended legs, especially when dangling, are some way to get sore legs. Closeness is high on this one; you're face-to-face and you can enjoy passionate kissing while you're at it. My advice is that you best enjoy this one slowly. DSS is high, but also depends on your frame. Larger frame makes access a bit more of a challenge, but this can be compensated for by the flexibility of the wife's legs. The stimulation is in the hands of the wife here, she sets the speed and the force of landing.

- **Standing positions**

Standing positions, especially ones that require the husband to carry his wife during the act, are good for quickies. I don't think one can go for hours with his wife against the wall. Other variations of standing are derivatives of the above, like rear-entry while the wife leans over a chair/table or other object. The premise is that both or one of the spouses are standing during the sex. This may even involve oral sex, with the wife sitting on a table while the husband kneels, or the reverse happens with a kneeling wife and standing husband.

The beauty of standing positions is that they increase our range of motion and usually decrease the pressure we apply with our body weight over our spouses. The downside is that some are not that deep in terms of DSS, but this can be circumvented with a bit of creativity. For example, rear-entry while standing may pose a challenge of height, so using an aerobic stepper could be a good way to elevate the one spouse and alter the angle of entry and the DSS by extension. You must remember, small changes can make the biggest difference in sex.

Ratings: Longevity 7.5/10, Closeness 5/10, DSS 5/10... The high longevity is for the reasons explained above, with the downside being that some standing positions require the husband to carry his wife. The closeness and DSS are a 50/50 because it depends on the exact positions, your height and level of fitness. Usually though, you may have to sacrifice closeness for a higher DSS.

- **Self-made position**

I can write an entire book about positions, but that will not replace the need for each couple to find their positon. Having 2 or 3 go-to positions form the list above is great. But every now and again, get into the habit of enjoying sex differently. Try something new, or get creative and collaborate with your spouse in designing a new position of your own with props of your choosing. The point is to get into the habit of altering positions to alter your experiences. Just be mindful that no one gets injured and consider getting in shape to widen the scope of your repertoire. There are no ratings for this position because it is one of your making, in fact you could give it a 10 all-round, or less than that. It is yours, you do with it what you will.

I hope you are not caught up in the names that you miss the point. Some of these names may be offensive, or less than churchy, but the idea is that you have a clear mental picture of the position by using a name that you are likely to have come across in the past. Frankly, all names are made up and they are used as references to invoke mental pictures for purpose of communication.

Location and Sex Furniture

I was once a member of a WhatsApp group for married Christian couples and a discussion about whether each person felt comfortable having sex at their in-law's house was being had. The contributions were quite hilarious, most of which leaned towards doing it quick and doing it quietly. It made me wonder what kind of environments could you comfortably have sex? This is where the idea of furniture pieces being designed and used for sex. I also find the concept of sex furniture to be fascinating because certain pieces of general furniture are viewed as possible locations of exploration.

I am typically perceived as an introverted person who likes to keep to himself. Writing this book alone breaks the mould for me in more ways than one. I've been fairly consistent throughout the years and this demeanour of mine was a cause for concern for my wife. Shortly after our wedding, she confessed to have been concerned that I would be 'too nice' in matters sexual and that my demeanour outside the bedroom would be directly translated to a less than exciting time in the sack. I'm pleased to report that she has not complained a single time. Part of this is down to keeping an open mind about the where, when and how of sex. Specifically relating to the 'where', there are no rules on this but general principles for identifying a great spot include these considerations:

    i. **Privacy**

Privacy is two-pronged. First, when you are in a private space, you are unlikely to be disturbed before, during and after sex. There are little to no distractions to getting your game on. The second aspect is that privacy implies an exclusivity that is unlikely to disturb others. An example is a married couple enjoying sex in their own house where they live alone, versus doing so in a packed house at one of their in-laws. You want to be able to enjoy sex without the worry of someone walking into you in the act. In fact, this worry will be at the back of your mind and divide your attention, which is bad news for your sexual experience. On the other hand, having sex at a place like this may be thrilling because the likelihood of being found-out adds a dimension of adventure to the act, i.e. doing it in the bathroom while everyone else thinks you're getting ready and using the bathroom concurrently to speed things up.

i. **Comfort**.

This is related to the act itself. Sex should never be uncomfortable (at least after you get used to it). Wherever you're doing it from, you should be at ease and relaxed enough for it to be enjoyable. This is where the furniture or location on which sex is being had is important. A comfortable bed will make a huge difference in your enjoyment of sex. Some people fantasise about sex on the couch, but a hard couch will do more damage than good. There are other objects of furniture that people use to have sex on, i.e. chairs, ottomans, etc... the idea is that the furniture should allow you to enjoy the sexual act in a manner that is both comfortable and private. A squeaky bed will tell on you and likely be uncomfortable if you have guest or people in the other room(s) of your place.

It is also worth noting the importance of being realistic, you cannot reasonably expect a piece of flimsy furniture that would likely struggle to carry one person to carry a load of two moving persons. You don't want to risk injury. Use sturdy, yet comfortable furniture on which to perform your sexual acts. My advice is simple, when in doubt, use your bed. There are thousands of variations that you can enjoy on a comfortable bed with minimal risk of injury. You don't want that steamy sex in the shower (excuse the pun) to turn into a call to the emergency room after a slip-and-break incident.

i. Sex Furniture

Here, as in anything less than 'ordinary', the idea of using furniture pieces is one that requires conversation between a married couple. This is because any reservations may hinder your ability to enjoy yourself while using such items. What you want to have is mutual consent and oneness of mind while using any apparatus during sex. There are specific pieces designed for sex in particular. I won't go into these here, rather, my focus is on the need for cultivating an open mind when approaching the use of these during sex. Again, if anyone is uncomfortable with this, it is best that it is not used.

You may be interested in using normal furniture and getting creative with its use. For example, the straddle on a seat position above is one where a chair can be used as sex furniture. Someone close to me recommended this as a means of adding some spice to our sexual repertoire. Another very common item for use is the couch/sofa. In the right setting, it can take on a different use depending on your requirements. It can literally replace your bed. One other item is a table, this provides great elevation for acts such as oral sex, or even a steamy foreplay of your own creation. The point here is that anything can be used as a locus for sex, provided that it is consensual, and no harm is done to either participants. I must reiterate the issue of safety, you do not want to call *911* after a mishap on a less-than-sturdy table; it may be funny in hindsight, but never great in the moment... and no, I do not speak from experience...lol.

The ideal after-sex position

The popular idea of sex is a man on top of a woman, grinding away as they enjoy their sexual encounter all night long. Little to no consideration is given to what happens after sex. First, sex is messy. So, get some towels or other articles to use to clean-up after sex. Especially when you have had one of those flowing romps where juices flow all over; you need to clean-up. Before you do, be mindful of the emotional element of sex.

Some of us enter into our marriage having had a history with sex, and a notably bad one. A history where our bodies were used to fulfil the other persons' lustful desires and the whole act of sex was tainted with shame and regret. So jumping out of bed and rushing into a shower after sex may communicate a message that sends your spouse straight to their life before Christ and even before you, for others, it may not even be that detailed, simply jumping out of bed and carrying on as if nothing happened may communicate neglect and imply that you are going on about life now that you have gotten what you want. This is especially true for women, most women want to cuddle after sex as this reassures them (on a subconscious level) that their man is not just in it for the body, but he also cares about her person holistically. The cuddles are also a response to the flow of attachment hormones that tend to flow after sex.

The idea is to be transparent with your spouse about how you'd like to act after sex. Although this may seem like over planning and contrary to the popular idea that sex is this spontaneous explosion of passion devoid of any forethought. After learning how you and your spouse feel post sex, you will understand that talking things through and changing your behaviour so that it communicates love and affection before, during and after sex is more important than your long-held notions of what sex is. My recommendation, which is what we did from our early days in marriage, is that you chat about how the sex was, i.e., what you liked, and what you felt through each moment. This discussion should happen organically as you get used to it, but it should never be a platform for vile criticism of the other. Focus on what you liked and give a bit of guidance on what or how you want to be pleasured. Also pay the same attention to what your spouse gives you as feedback. My experience has been that when I focus on pleasuring my wife according to how she wants to be pleasured, it gives me pleasure and she's likely to reciprocate based on my feedback. This creates an endless cycle of servitude in the 'marriage bed'- an absolute wonder.

Changing the narrative

Sex is usually perceived as something driven by men. But *oh,* the pleasures of woman-led sex... Every Christian man I know who's dared to share anything about their life in marriage, and their sex life in particular raves about those moments when their wife just grabs them and takes matters into her own hands. There's something doubly arousing for us men when we are being desired by our wives in this way.

I saw an article in the editorial section of a local newspaper where a commentator was pleading with women to get on top of their men. The commentator spelled put the benefits, but chief among them is the thrill of being taken by the hand and led into sexual adventure by your wife. The stereotype is that we men are the sex thirsty among the married. So, a reversal of this now and again is such a thrill. Ladies, if you haven't already, I call on you to give it a try. Get home before your husband, prepare him a meal, and find out when he'll arrive and run him a bath. Serve him his food and have him wash up before you gift him the best sex he's had yet. Treat him like a king. He will be infinitely grateful and will be smiling all day the next day. Change the narrative that men should always initiate sex, men get so much slack out there, it is wonderful to be treated like royalty now and again, trust me, I know it all too well.

You may notice that the positions outlined here are very lean on the use of devices and toys. This is deliberate. I find that using toys is something that most couples need to graduate to, if ever. Secondly, the idea of toys always divides attention, in that the toy can become the focus and not the partner with whom you are enjoying sex. However, this does not preclude you from making use of them as you see fit. The key is to adequately communicate this with your spouse and ensure that you both do something that sits well with **both** of you. Remember, it takes two to tango.

Another aspect of the positions presented above is how both parties need to play an active role in sex. There is no room for 'spring chickens' in a lively sex life. Use your hands, move your hips, do something. This is not a rule, but it is a principle. Sometimes, it is good to sit back and let your spouse do their thing. Most times, you need to get in the game holistically and take an active role. This is how you make sex what it should be; the two becoming one.

In *Chapter 2*, we dealt with the idea that sex is a matter of the mind. Having covered the aspect of sex positions, let us get back to the mind and delve into sexual fantasies.

Chapter 4: Sexual Fantasies

In this chapter we turn our attention the idea of sexual fantasies. We'll build upon our understanding that sex happens in the mind, as covered in chapter 2. This means that whatever becomes of one's sexual life is the manifestation of some idea they've had in the past, so that there is nothing really spontaneous about sex. It may be in the moment, but it is always preconceived. Our thoughts or preconceptions have so much power that they can make or break our sex lives. In fact, what often hinders a great sex life in marriage is rooted in our thoughts. However, this is not going to be our focus, what we will consider is the type of thoughts we have concerning sex and how we could deal with these in our marriage. We'll also consider the *fantasy of all fantasies* which we **all** need to aspire to.

In exploring the locus of sex in chapter 2, we dealt with the issue of the mind-body-spirit diagram (a.k.a. the trichotomy of man diagram). In this diagram, you will remember that the mind is parted three ways. All of the elements that make up the mind are key to understanding your sexual fantasies and those of your spouse. If your spouse is like me, rationalising everything and going through life this way, their fantasies may be stronger on the "intellect" element and weaker in the other two. If, like my wife, your spouse is stronger on the emotional side, then their fantasies will lean towards being fulfilling in an emotional way. As discussed in *Chapter 2*, the will is largely influenced by the intellect and emotions when it comes to sex, however a basic **will**ingness to partake in the other's fantasy is a great starting point. So, in order to fully appreciate a sexual fantasy, one needs to understand their spouse's fantasy from the perspective of their strengths and mind-set. Being cautious not to violate themselves in the interest of partaking in the other's fantasy.

Porn

It is impossible to write anything meaningful about sex without the mention of porn. Its inclusion in a chapter on sexual fantasies may not be surprising but the 'how' and 'why' it would be in this book might. Consuming[15] porn is a particularly a destructive habit because it does so much damage to your mind that your thoughts (and eventually your actions) relating to sex, marriage and family are distorted. A serious case of porn addiction may require specific medical and/or psychological attention. Let's deal with it from the perspective of how and why it impacts marriage sex[16].

The simple truth is that not many of us make it to full adulthood without exposure to porn. The statistics on this are well documented. In 2009, Michael Leahy released results of a survey of 29,000 individuals at North American universities (Covenant Eyes, 2020):

- 51% of male students and 32% of female students first viewed pornography before their teenage years (12 and younger).
- 35% of all students' first exposure was Internet or computer-based (compared to 32% from magazines, 13% from VHS or DVD, and 18% from Cable or pay-per-view).
- 64% of college men and 18% of college women spend time online for Internet sex every week.
- 42% of male students and 20% of women said they regularly read romance novels, sexually explicit magazines, or regularly visited sexually explicit websites or chat rooms.

A few observations from this research is that it is a bit old, given that it was published in 2009 when the internet was not so popular among the youth, and the social media buzz was not yet buzzing. Though some may question its relevance because of how old it is, it is scary to think that our present-day situation is likely much worse. Search anything on the internet and you're bound to walk into some degree of porn (what is often referred to as soft porn). From revealing pictures of people posting themselves on social media platforms, to explicit content presented in words, or a wordplay as part of an ad' campaign. Avoiding sexual/adult content is very difficult these days.

Another observation is that society seems to be heading in a direction where we're conditioned for consumption of adult content from our preteen years.

It's no wonder that some major studios are focused on adding LGBTQIA+ content in cartoons. Get them young, and get them fast, for good- this seems to be the strategy. Prior to the era in which the research was done, young people (especially boys) consumed porn on playboy magazines, or the like. These days, it's at their fingertips via smart devices. It's also frightening to realise how in the past, our view of what was pornographic or 'unsavoury' was much stricter than today. Think of how the fashion world has been influenced by our changing culture and the purported views on body positivity. For me, I always get back to Adam and Eve's covering of their bodies in shame after the fall, and how we are doing the revers; it's as if we are celebrating nakedness these days.

Perhaps an obvious observation from the above is the gap that exists in porn use when comparing males to their female counterparts. Why? Because the eye-gate is where we men are weakest. Put differently, the gateway to attraction in men is through the eyes. {Aside} This is often misrepresented as a 'factory fault' in us men, but I speak for us all when I say this could be leveraged by our wives to up the ante in our sex lives. Make of this what you will, but if anything, pursue visual attractiveness for your husband. While this is subjective, find out from him what **he likes**. Women get caught up in pursuing what they like regardless of what their husbands like. This is not a misogynistic point, but I speak from experience. If a woman wants to attract her husband and keep him attracted to her, she must do so in a means that is attractive **for him.**

A few key points about Porn and its possible effects on people who are addicted to it...

- Addiction

All the above and other stats indicate that we're primed for addiction to sexual content from a young age. This doesn't have to start intentionally, but graduation in that direction is guaranteed when you start young. The problem with children's minds is that they do not have the ability to discern, that ability develops over time with experience and wisdom. Unfortunately, when habits of consuming sexual content are begun in early youth, they normalise something that is destructive. You see, the goal of the enemy is not to convince you that it is good to watch porn. It is to convince you that it is normal to do so. The difference between these targets is that the one is a matter of conviction, the other a matter of perspective. Satan doesn't need to have us in sin, he just has to have us doubt our position in purity.

- Is it right?

Asking this is asking the wrong question. What we should consider is what the consequences are and not the correctness of our actions. Much of our evaluation in life is black-and-white, right/wrong, hot/cold... All contrasts, weighing one thing against another; be it a standard, culture, or ideal. But the idea of right and wrong is definitive, in that we seek to do what is right or we avoid the wrong without being clear about the consequences of each course of action. I propose that you focus on the consequences and let that guide you on the correctness of consuming porn content. This is not an original idea, remember when Jesus taught us how to identify false prophets? He said we will know them by their fruits. A fruit is a consequence/outcome of the biological operation of a tree, so that a good tree will bring forth good fruit, and a bad one, bad fruit. Let's consider the consequences of consuming pornographic content:

According to the Journal of Adolescent Health, prolonged exposure to pornography leads to (Covenant Eyes, 2020):

- An **exaggerated perception** of sexual activity in society.
- Diminished trust between intimate couples.
- The abandonment of the hope of sexual monogamy.
- Belief that promiscuity is the natural state.
- Belief that abstinence and sexual inactivity are unhealthy.
- Cynicism about love or the need for affection between sexual

partners.
- **Belief that marriage is sexually confining.**
- **Lack of attraction to family and child-raising.**

According to sociologist Jill Manning, the research indicates pornography consumption is associated with the following six trends, among others (Covenant Eyes, 2020):

1. Increased marital distress, and risk of separation and divorce.
2. Decreased marital intimacy and sexual satisfaction.
3. Infidelity.
4. Increased appetite for more graphic types of pornography and sexual activity associated with abusive, illegal or unsafe practices.
5. Devaluation of monogamy, marriage and child rearing.
6. An increasing number of people struggling with compulsive and addictive sexual behaviour.

The above findings have one target: destroying the nuclear family. If you succeed at doing this, society is broken. So porn is bad news for any marriage and if it is bad for marriage, it is bad for anyone.

- Should we use it as inspiration?

There are strong proponents of the idea that nothing is wrong on an absolute basis, and that all things are relative. True as this may be for many topics of discussion, it sadly doesn't apply to porn. Porn is destructive to the people who create it as much as it is to the people who consume it. This is why my response to a question of whether it is worth using porn as a form of inspiration in married sex is simply this: **get creative with your spouse, and only with your spouse. Stay away from porn.** I don't think anything more is worth using to convince you of the dangers of this addictive habit other than what I have laid out above. If you are still not convinced, I challenge you to do some reading on the industries that are linked to the production of porn, i.e., child and human trafficking, drug trade and many more ills that involve crimes against humanity. Sure, very few industries can be considered to be 100% 'clean' but knowing that the consumption of porn is destructive to yourself and the lives of so many others is a serious case of infringement of the commandment of loving thy neighbour.

I've taken the time to write about porn because it is such a dangerous form of content. The dangers are spelled out above, but in the main, it is to destroy people, society and culture. If we remember John 10:10, we will note that the enemy comes to steal, kill and destroy. In porn, what he steals, kills and destroys is family. If you've had a run-in with addiction to porn, there is hope, because Jesus follows up this statement in John 10:10 by saying this; "I came that they may have life and have it abundantly." Among other things, what Jesus meant when He said life was a liberation from oppression and bondage. He came to do the reverse of what Satan does. In fact, Satan is the anti-Christ, and he does the opposite of what God does. Jesus came to restore what Satan has stolen. He came to regenerate and resurrect what Satan has killed. And he came to re-build what has been destroyed. Isn't our Lord Wonderful, isn't this the greatest news in history?

The kicker is that the renewal of the mind is possible in Jesus Christ. We can be regenerated, and we are given a new hope in Christ. You may have been plagued by the addiction to porn in the past, you may be on your way to recovery. I do not know what it has cost you, but what I know is that it is no match for the power of the Lord Jesus Christ. The word assured us that we are new creations in Christ (2Cor5v17). The old passes away and behold the new. Along with the old goes our failures and short comings, as we are ushered into a new life of abundance. We also have the support of brothers and sisters willing to aid us in learning how to stay on the 'straight and narrow' as far as porn is concerned. I would recommend checking out CovenantEyes™ on their website[17] and the resources they have to offer. There are other credible resources that can help you; seek these and you may yet find revival.

Can Christians be Naughty?

Sex was never designed to be churchy. What I mean by this is that there aren't standardised rules about how to go about it, how often should you do it, and where it should be done. There is, however, one rule that the word stipulates concerning married sex... "Let marriage be held in honour among all, and let the marriage bed be undefiled, for God will judge the sexually immoral and adulterous (Hebrews 13:4 ESV)" The truth is that God will judge us for how we treat the gift of marriage and married sex. We are called to honour marriage, this means that we should all treat it with respect and hold it in high regard in speech and in deed, especially our own marriage. We should also see to it that we do not set conditions or an environment that would be conducive to the defiling of the marriage bed. This includes an avoidance of flirting and 'hitting' on people of the other gender who are not your spouse. We men are susceptible to this, as our level of attractiveness tends to rise the moment, we get married. This is because married men are seen to be dependable, mature and less of a hassle in extra-marital affairs because they do their thing and get back to their wives and family. This is not the biblical conduct we're called to.

To answer the question of whether Christians can be naughty, I think one has to define naughty. If naughty involves anything outside the confines of honour and fidelity concerning your marriage, then **NO! YOU SHOULD NOT BE NAUGHTY.** That isn't to say you should not be adventurous and that you should not enjoy a wonderful sex life with your spouse, because sex is such a wonderful gift of God to the married, in fact I like to think of sex as playtime for adults. It's exciting, unpredictable and something to be enjoyed with a loving partner. What I also believe about sex is that it is much more exciting with one partner. All this talk about having extra-marital affairs, sex with 2+ people at once is all a design by the enemy to pollute and pervert what God has masterfully designed. Sex with one partner frees you of insecurity, because you're less focused on 'performing well' when you're confident that your spouse loves you and is enjoying this gift with you in love. You're also not looking over your shoulder in guilt because there's something intrinsically 'right' about sex with your spouse. Sex within the confines of marriage removes all doubt, because you're not constantly worried about what you spouse 'has' in the way of disease. In a sense, you commit your life to each other, and each spouse's fidelity is a protection of themselves and their spouse. Lastly, my experience has been that it gets better with time and proper communication, two things that aren't synonymous with extra-marital affairs and 2+ sexual engagements.

Arguing that married sex is boring and placing value in breaking fidelity and honour in marriage is short-sighted. God, the masterful and majestic designer and creator of this world also created sex. There's an entire book in the bible that speaks about married sex, so clearly it is something of importance to Him that we enjoy ourselves in the 'marriage bed'. However, this comes with the responsibility to safeguard it with fidelity and honour. We therefore have to be mindful that everything we do in our sex lives as couples glorifies God by conforming to the scripture. To borrow a line from spider-man "with great power, comes great responsibility", and our responsibility is to glorify God in all that we do, even in our sex lives.

BDSM – Bondage & Discipline, Domination & Submission

Some people may have entered the faith having read or watched movies based on the concept of BDSM. What is BDSM you may wonder? It refers to Bondage, Discipline, Domination and Submission. This is when a couple engages in sexplay that errs on the side of aggression and permissive violence. This may involve striking with various objects (i.e., whipping), chaining or binding and even other unsanitary practices like passing human excrement on the personage of the other (yes, golden showers are real). But is it something worth having among Christians? Here's my take.

BDSM, as you might deduce is an acronym that doesn't align with the actual wording. It should be BDMS, but I guess the current acronym sounds better. In BDSM, one can also put in sadism and masochism. With sadism being the tendency to derive pleasure by inflicting pain or humiliation to others. While masochism refers to deriving pleasure from inflicting pain or humiliating oneself. Some people just brush this off as a kinky fetish, but defining it is enough to send your internal alarm bells ringing.

When this sub-category of sexual literature was first thrust into mainstream media, it created a lot of buzz. Some saw no harm in it because the dominant male had the consent of the submissive female. In other instances, the roles were reversed. But others did not take too kindly to it because it bordered on violence. So, the question is where should the Church stand on this? What does the Word say?

I could quote the *golden rule*[18], but that would have the loophole of consent, and a willingness from the 'dominant' to revert to 'submissive'. Proponents of BDSM 'preach' informed consent, as if my consenting to my own murder absolves the hired killer of the responsibility for killing me... Consent does not alter the substance of the sexual act. I could talk about the violence perpetrated by the dominant and supporters of such would argue it is not violence if the submissive consents and has a 'safe word'... the arguments for this practice can be compelling. But my take is simple, and it centres on the question of *what is the source of this behaviour?* Why would anyone want to exercise dominion over another? That doesn't seem to be a Christ-like spirit. When we were designed by God in Genesis 1:26, he wanted us to have dominion <u>over the earth</u>, not each other. Further, He wants us to submit to Him and His word, not to the domination of others. Therefore, my view is that a desire to engage in domination of your spouse or to be subjugated should be interrogated. My laymen opinion is that you need to deal with matters of your heart. Maybe a past experience of being violated has led you to a fetish for dominating others. On the other hand, a desire to be subjugated under your own terms may be an attempt of gaining control by guided subjugation and doing so by your own terms. I will not even talk about humiliation and inflicting pain. We must remember that our bodies are temples of the Holy Spirit, and so are the bodies of our spouses... so why would you want to inflict pain or even subject the temple of the Holy Ghost to humiliation? We'll tackle this and other elements of our past that tend to creep into our marriages and sex lives in Chapter 6. But the bottom-line is that BDSM should not be found among believers. Any behaviour of that sort is not fitting of a professing Christian.

Let Sacrifice be your Fantasy!

It must be weird reading that sub-heading, having the word sacrifice and fantasy in the same line. The idea that sacrifice can be fantastic is absurd, but it isn't, because you cannot have great sex if you're selfish, and sacrifice usually demands a denial of self. Now I must say there's a difference between sacrifice and self-destructive behaviour. Knowing the difference is important, because so many people end up hurt because they think they are sacrificing (denying themselves) for the greater good of a collective when in fact they are self destructing.

One of the most important pieces of advice I received before marriage was from a friend of mine who said: "don't come before she does". Embedded in this advice was the idea that my enjoyment in sex should not come before that of my wife. This isn't to say that she's more important than I am in the equation. However, this is the mind-set I needed to have in order to remove focus from 'me' and participate in her reaching her satisfaction. The lessons I learnt from applying this advice are simple, but quite profound.

i. When my focus was on participating in my wife's enjoyment, I realised that I felt less pressure to perform, but I was willing to listen more to what she had to offer in guiding me for her maximum pleasure. I wasn't without fault or error, but all the feedback did not feel like an attack, rather a course-correction towards becoming a better sexual partner. Inadvertently, I became better at listening because I was now able to handle a topic as sensitive as my performance with grace and kindness for both parties involved.

ii. The other thing I realised was that when I removed attention from my own enjoyment, and fixed my eyes on serving her, I somehow enjoyed the experience more. Seeing and being a part of her experience, a wonderful time was doubly satisfying to me. I was killing two birds with one stone; I was satisfying my wife and myself.

iii. A mind-set of service insulates you from taking advantage of your spouse. I am not talking rape here, but I note the tendency of sexual conversation in the secular space of leaning toward the male having the time of his life, or a woman getting what she deserves. However, marriage is about meeting each other's needs. So, when both spouses take the approach of serving each other sexually, the result is often a 'fight' to serve the other and not strife to get what each person wants. Be warned, sometimes this can result in explosive encounters of blissful pleasure- for both parties.

Great sex is the product of sacrificial, mutual service to the other's needs. The institution of marriage is unique in that the husband is called to love his wife, and the wife is called to submit to the husband. Interestingly, they are both called to do what the other is naturally prone to doing. It is easy to see how women find it easy to love. Women tend to be nurturers, caregivers and lovers. They're also more easily attuned to their emotions than their male counterparts. I see this in how patient and loving my wife is with our son; I would never be able to operate at her level in parenting[19]. So, a command to love would seem better suited to women than men, but not for God and His infinite wisdom. Though it can be argued that the tendency of women toward love has submission embedded in it, a closer look would suggest otherwise. If we look back at the judgement of God on Eve following the fall (I don't like calling it a curse), you'd notice that God pronounced that Eve's desire shall be for her husband. This is not sexual, but it regards the woman vying for the authority of the man. Lurking within them, because of sin is the proneness to this behaviour. I suppose this is because the fall was a result of the enemy's guile, and tricking Eve (a woman) to believing in lack even though there was none. Back in Genesis, the serpent tricked Eve into thinking there was greater gain in eating from the forbidden tree rather than enjoying all the **other** trees in the garden. Imagine this, if you are told to dine on everything except for on tree, are you lacking in anything?

On the other hand, the man's call to love also seems ordinary, given how romanticised our view of marriage and love are these days. However, it is not easy to fulfil this call because we men are typically more adept to our rationality than our emotional side. One of the ways we see this idea of how men easily fall into submission out of a sense of duty, than they are to love is in war. Men would give their lives in submission to a king and leave their wives and children to follow him to fight selfish wars out of a sense of duty. Sure, they may claim to be doing this 'For God and Country', but it is their sense of duty that seems to be active here rather than love in the typical sense of love.

In the end, we are all called to doing what goes against our intrinsic abilities, when we do this, we are living in sacrificial love and the outcome is a wonderful illustration of Christ and the church. How does this play into our marriage bed? Simple, when we love sacrificially outside the bedroom, taking that into it becomes less of a strain and great sex is much more probable in such an environment.

Finally, you may wonder why this chapter does not include any explicit exposition of a particular sexual fantasy. Further, you may question the reason I haven't given specific guidelines for creating a fantasy. All this is not coincidental. The fact is that all our sexual experiences are unique to us as couples. Another fact is that I would not let myself try to do something God chose not to do- that is to have specific prescriptions for and about married sex. I believe that we've been given the gift of sex to enjoy as we see fit within marriage. However, we have been given a responsibility to abide by the guidelines of honour and fidelity. Honour is due to God for the grace He's shown in His giving us this and other gifts. Honour is due also to our spouses and the covenant of marriage we have entered into, not only as a gift but a privilege we've been given to portray Christ and the Church. Fidelity is due, as we are supposed to protect our spouse from hurt by infidelity. Speaking of fidelity, I like to simplify it by borrowing the words of Jesus in the Sermon on the Mount: "*So whatever you wish that others would do to you, do also to them, for this is the Law and the Prophets* (Matthew 7:12 ESV)"

So be it in speech, thought or in deeds, do to your spouse what you wish they would do to you. I've seen this among guys growing up, there's a huge emphasis on the weakness of men concerning women. This normalises the promiscuity and having casual sex (at least among non-Christians). Yet in my conversations with men who think like this, many of them condemn a woman who would do the same. They are like the men who wanted to stone the woman caught 'red-handed', only that they cast the stone regardless of their own hearts.

Chapter 5: In the Act

Pleasure over Performance

Our culture is geared for performance, efficiency and convenience. Our cars are designed this way- they have to give our most *power*, using the *least resources* to provide the greatest *convenience*. Other products are no different- food, fashion, devices, media... the list is endless. The same goes for our hypersexualised culture. It has indoctrinated us with the view that we ought to perform during sex (pun intended). It's all about *power*. We've also been taught that sex is effortless and should be spontaneous and wild (least resources). Of course, it should be convenient. The thing about convenience though is that it is self-serving. Anytime you want something to be convenient, it is usually serving *you*. Unfortunately, this attitude doesn't bode well in married sex.

The issue with this view on sex is that it is often self-serving. When a man cares more about his performance than the pleasure of his wife, he can go on for hours while his wife is in pain. The cries are also likely to be interpreted for moans... *disaster*. The same goes for a wife who wants to scream the foundations apart to give her husband the impression of enjoyment- it comes at a cost of genuine pleasure. For both parties, who wants to be pretentious with their spouse anyway? Putting up an image of pleasure while you're in pain is what I call the Façade Ideology.

The other problem with 'performance' in the stereotypical sense is that it is one of those concepts that seems to permeate culture without being truly defined. If I asked 10 people what performance is in a sexual context, I would get 10 different responses? Worse so when I blend male and female in this test group. This is dangerous, because and undefined concept with such a universal appeal is often a set-up for disappointments and heartbreak. The vague view of what performance is includes but is not limited to: the ability to make your partner squirm and orgasm, the ability to last long where the long is not defined either. The vague view of performance loosely involves the frequency of sex- that is having a lot of sex, which is also undefined. Performance also refers to having total control over what proceeds during sex, and it is usually male-dominant; that is, the focus is on men to perform and drive sexual encounters. All this causes undue pressure and makes the whole thing less than what it is. Mutuality should be at the heart of sex, mutual love, mutual understanding and mutual engagement in all that takes place during sex. What that means is that the quality, frequency and overall state of your sex life is the responsibility of both spouses. You both define and live out what you've defined your sex life should be. What's also important to remember is that sex is about pleasure, not performance[20]. In fact, true performance during and after sex is the result of pleasure. So, when we pursue pleasuring our spouses we inadvertently perform, whatever we may define that to be.

Intimate Conversation

The façade ideology plagues society in every area. Ask anyone how they are doing, and 90% of the time the response will be 'good'... but is it really good? Divorce rates, suicide rates and the amount of people checking into mental institutions on account of depression suggests otherwise. It is our responsibility as Christians, especially in our marriages, to be transparent to our spouses. This is where intimacy is key, because it allows the other to get close and into their spouse's inner circle. A place where you're always up to date with their internal state of affairs. This is the foreground for honest communication on what brings us pleasure and what causes us pain.

Conversations on sex are always difficult at the start, but using strategies that make it less taboo will not only make it easier to talk sex, but greatly improve your sex life also. A great place to start is to remove the barriers and initiate the conversation by asking the relevant questions:

- What gives you the most pleasure?
- What causes you the most pain?
- Talk me through your best sexual experience ever.
- Talk me through your worst experience ever?

Following these up with further probing conversation, while reassuring your spouse that their response is not being taken personally will likely improve the quality of the feedback you get. Another tip would be to sit together and write the responses to these questions before discussion it (you can even go into separate rooms and record audio if writing is a problem for you). When you get back together, you can discuss your responses, as this will avoid you becoming defensive about your spouse's feedback before they get to lay out the full response.

A lot on communication and tips are covered in chapter 2 along with Chapter 8 and Chapter 10. But now that we've laid a foundation on communication, let's get into *the act*.

Let's Get Physical

I know I said sex happens in the mind (chapter 2), but sex involves physical interaction. I'm sure you've heard of phone sex, sexting and the like. However, the *real* thing happens with that involvement of physical touch, usually involving genitals. A great place to start is to have a basic understanding of the sexual anatomy.

- **Sexual anatomy**- a *watered down version*

  Understanding the anatomy of your spouse is essential in gaining the ability to pleasure them. This is not to mean that you should attend a biology class specifically for sex, although this might not be the worst of ideas. A simple understanding of the makings of each other's bodies is always a plus.

  Firstly, both husband and wife should concede that the other's body is different to theirs. Second, you must be clear that among our own genders, we are different. Some people like gentle strokes to get them aroused, while others prefer the touch to be a bit firmer. It's like going for a massage, a good masseuse will ask you to choose how firm you want them to apply pressure as they massage you.

I will not go into the details here, nor will I bore you with the scientific jargon or lingo. Simply, there are areas of our bodies that are erogenous in nature; that means that touching of these areas results in arousal and sexual pleasure. It is important to note that arousal and sexual pleasure are not mutually exclusive, however, they are different. Arousal refers to a state of heightened sensation to sexually inclined touching/speaking. Words can cause arousal just as much as touching. A combination of these two modes of communication is even better. An example of arousal is the typical hardening of male genitalia when touched by the wife, or when the idea of sex is spoken of. For women, arousal may take the form of hardened nipples, goose bumps, throbbing of certain areas of the body and moistening of the genital area. The idea is that we're all different, and trying different approaches may help in finding what is best for your spouse.

Sexual pleasure on the other hand, refers to the pleasure derived from sexual action- be it physical or non-physical. The physical is easy to grasp, but non-physical may be a bit of a curveball for some. Simply, non-physical sexual pleasure can include the sharing of pictures, texts, or even a steamy voice call telling your spouse about things to come when you meet again later. The big takeaway though is that arousal precedes sexual pleasure, so that there is no sexual pleasure without arousal.

Typically, men are quite easy to get to arousal. One touch in a sexual way and the 'man down there' stands to attention. There are exceptions to this for various reasons, but generally, this is how it goes for most of us. For the women, more care and attention are required to get them aroused and ready to enjoy sexual pleasures. This involves a solid foundation of meeting her emotional needs and having a great relationship outside of sex. This may not seem like a very important aspect, but it serves as the starting point for great sex. I was listening to a gentleman contrast the arousal of women to that of men. He said men are like heating food in the microwave, a few seconds and the food is getting hot. It heats up very quickly the longer you keep it there. Women on the other hand are like that old coal-fired stove. It needs time to heat up and requires preparation before the fire even gets started. Now the biggest issues arise from this difference. Most men aren't willing to be patient enough to get their spouse to a point of arousal and readiness for sex. As a friend of mine put it- they just want to 'box it', comparing how men enter a sexual experience with the attitude of a boxer; full force and the round is over in 2-3 minutes, or less. You need to take time with the ladies, have them warm up well. As a rule of thumb, remember this adage- you can't float a boat on dry land. He who has ears, let him hear....

- **Pleasure spots**

We have different pleasure spots, but there are general ones that most people can respond to. By giving this list, I am hoping that it is not one you would put up for criticism and ridicule, but rather a consideration. Call it a starter list on places you may consider.

- Genitals: this is universal. Both men and women appreciate measured and intentional stimulation of their genitalia. For men, this involves stroking, kissing and even suckling (more on oral sex in chapter 7). For the women, the same is true, stroking, kissing and suckling. However, the key is to be guided by your spouse on the intensity of each action- so listen attentively and follow their ques. Most men miss what is called the clitoris; the small bean-shaped portion on the upper area of the vaginal entry. This spot has enough nerve endings to rival the hand. It is a superstar of sexual pleasure. Done right, clitoral stimulation is enough to result in orgasm for some women. Inside the vagina, there's a spot called the G-spot. This is a spongy area that is accessible when the wife is 'wet', and a finger is inserted and moved in a 'come-hither' motion.

- Breasts.... Another area that doesn't get the attention it deserves. Breasts are so wonderful. They serve as carriers of nutrition for babies, and they also serve a wonderful sexual function for arousal. Done right, they too can result in orgasm and hot sexual stimulation I will let you and your spouse explore the 'how' part.

- Skin: this is a broad category, but this includes the variation of sensations on the skin. Hot/cold, wet/oily/dry contact... all I will say is that a lot of stroking of various areas is good news for arousal. Our hands are wonderful devices for sending our spouses into sexual bliss.

- Neck/behind the ears: This is for the women, kissing to the neck and a light variation of biting with the lips and licking can result in some of the hottest blood rushes for the women. This is thanks to the many nerve endings found in this area, and its proximity to the brain.

- Feet: A home-style massage done right is a sure way to bring arousal.

- Inner thighs: this is also for the women, another common place for arousal. I would suggest some tantalising motion towards the vaginal area in touch, kiss and stroking.

- Stomach/belly-button area

- Back and buttocks: spanking is a universal act of expressing sexual arousal or interest.

- Kissing: believe it or not, kissing can contribute positively to the intensity of arousal. Don't just peck kiss, become better at kissing. The one thing about kissing is that it can be integrated with stroking and stimulation of other areas with the hands. Remember to avoid doing too much at once, you don't want to redirect focus into multi-tasking and miss out on being in the moment and experiencing the pleasure.

- **Penetration**

This is usually the phase of the sex dance that most are familiar with. It often ends soon for some because of the intensity. In other instances, the entry comes too soon, and the end result is pain and discomfort. The simple and sage advice stands here; you can't float a boat on dry land. That is, never penetrate when dry. Dryness can result from a number of things, including health related matters and some medications may cause vaginal dryness. But generally, dryness down there is an indicator of something that likely requires professional medical attention. However, in a fix there are solutions, in fact one major solution- lubricant. Now I understand that we have different sensitivities to various products, but a good quality lubricant that caters for sensitive skin should do. They even have these in sachets for on-the-go romps. But in my experience, lubricant does not replace the women ability to moisten on their own, but in a simple line, the wetter the better.

Another less popular aspect of penetration is the need to penetrate when the penis stands to attention fully. In some positions, this may be a bit curvy, so be sure you're entering the right point, otherwise you may find yourself giggling at your silliness later on. I will not detail this any further but heed my advice.

Penetration is a phase of sexual intercourse worth enjoying. Be sure to check in with each other on how the other is doing, over time, this becomes less of a requirement, and you begin to have the ability to tell the winces of pain from the moans of pleasure. However, if anything feels painful- STOP!!! I cannot stress this enough. Your ability to enjoy sex in the moment is a down-payment for subsequent sexual encounters. Put differently, you are more likely to repeat an activity that you enjoyed than one you endured.

- **Oral sex**

This is one of those taboo areas of sex among Christian circles. Should a man and his wife engage in the act of using their mouths to stimulate each other's genitals? My response is two-fold. First, you have to do what you are both comfortable with. If either of you are not comfortable with the idea, then don't do it and if you are the one who proposes it and you spouse refuses, don't become negative and sulky about it. In truth, loving your spouse doesn't involve you getting what you want all the time, sometimes you have to love them sacrificially. In fact, when you show this understanding, it may be reciprocated with them changing over. The second element is an advocacy for the view of your mouth as part of your body, just like your genitalia. Couple this understanding with a willingness to try new things in the marriage bed; oral sex could be for you. There is obviously some precaution to be taken, chiefly, the precaution of maintaining good hygiene habits, and the avoidance of undue force. As a rule, trying new things should be something done slowly. How slowly? Whatever slow is for you, but slower.

- **Anal sex**

I will abuse my power on this one. Being the one writing, I will discourage it off the bat. Despite the precaution that can be taken to maintain hygiene, it has never been a good idea for me to try this. In fact, when we first spoke about our sex life, we were both in agreement that we would never try anal sex. Somehow it just irks us. If you are so inclined, give it a go and write to me on what it's like. If it is part of your repertoire, also write to me and let me know what it is like. However, penetration via the anus is a possibility from a physical perspective, but spiritually and emotionally, it just doesn't sit right with me.

Putting it all together: the **sexual bell curve**©

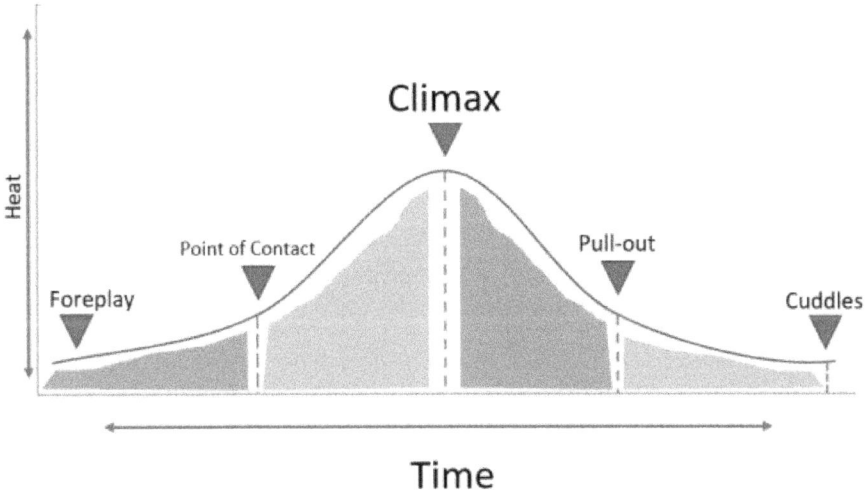

If you've ever seen a sex scene in a movie (which is highly likely if you watch movies these days), you will notice that very little communication happens during sex. In fact, most of our views on sex are based on movie sex. The sad thing about it is that movie sex is a fallacy. There's no foreplay, the couple having sex always seems clean afterwards, and they often fall asleep in the ensuing moments (or the scene cuts to the morning after). A lot of communication needs to happen during sex, but meaningful conversation. I've learnt that listening is better than asking/talking. Post sex clean up should ideally be a shared responsibility. Usually, the squirting that happens is heavier on the wife, so husbands can earn extra love points by helping their wives clean up. A bit of pre-prep may be necessary as well, with additional sheeting to 'catch the juices'[21]... If cuddling afterwards is your vibe – then cleanliness will be a trade-off and that's also okay if it is consensual. If you're new to sex, try both routes and see what works for you. You may even discover that having flushable wipes is a handy tool to clean up quickly before getting your cuddle on.

But before we get excited by the aftermath and clean-up stories, let's take the *sexual bell curve*® apart.

- **Foreplay**: this is the period in which you are both simmering. The heat level is not at its peak, but the idea and desire for sex is expressed by both parties. Now this is important, because in most cases it is the husband who is constantly chasing his wife, pleading for his sexual needs to be met. A word on this matter would simply be this- God created us differently, however in marriage we are both equipped with the resources we need to match the other's needs. So, if one spouse has a tendency toward a high sex drive, do not be dismayed, you both can, match each other if there is communication and patience of building up to a point where you meet each other sexually.

- **Point of contact**: this is the point where the husband penetrates his wife. I know, this could be part of the foreplay where the penetration happens using the fingers or mouth/tongue. However, for this illustration, I will assume penetration using genitalia. Here, the key is wetness, so men ought to be cautious not to 'go in' when it's dry, it causes pain and scarring/itchiness after. It's like running an engine without oil, it will get damaged and cost a fortune to fix/replace. In some instances, you could be in haste, so a word of advice- keep lube handy. As alluded to above, get a pack of sachets, so you can slide one into the pocket of your suit jacket for that impromptu romp at that black-tie event (it's amazing).

- **Climax**: Many women have never experienced climax during sexual intercourse. Why, you may ask? Well, for a number of reasons. One being that men sometimes climax too quickly. You see, for most men, the movement from foreplay, to point of contact and ultimately to climax could be seconds. The physiology of women, however, isn't created that way. They need sustained pressure and penetration at the right spot to reach climax. Enter the need for foreplay. Foreplay makes the transition much smoother and accelerates the wife's progression to climax. The tantalising, touching, word play (more on this in Chapter 7), all contribute to an environment where her mind is fully in the moment and makes it likely for her to reach climax, and even stay there.

- **Pull-out**: This is the moment where some may have issues. It is argued that men shouldn't pull-out right after ejaculation (which is synonymous with climax for men). This is because 'leaving it parked in her' is likely to sustain her climax, if you did so simultaneously. It's also a mind-thing, in that an immediate pull-out may communicate that you are done with what you came in for, and now you're going on about your own business. You see, the difference between casual sex and married sex is that in marriage, sex is about connecting at a level deeper than our bodies, casual sex is about enjoying each other's bodies, period. Casual sex is about release, married sex is about coming together. As always, my preference may not align to yours. So be adventurous, try both; pull-out right after ejaculation and try 'leaving it in' a few times. Then give each other feedback about what your individual experience was. Who knows, maybe you'd end up adding the pull-out or lack thereof in your repertoire of sexual manoeuvres.

- **Cuddles**: this is where most of us men get it wrong. Most times men are guilty of acting like sex ends when they ejaculate; it doesn't. The entire encounter is like a good workout. It begins with a warm-up (foreplay), the actual workout (point of contact), the muscle burn (climax), cool-down (pull-out) and the post-workout stretch (cuddles). If you miss the post-workout stretch, my experience is that it backfires the next morning and several days thereafter. Similarly, skipping the cuddles, especially when our spouse needs them is a disservice to a great sexual encounter. The cuddles are more for the emotional binding of the couple then they are about the sex. To add to an argument for adding this to your post-sex routine is that it can be viewed as foreplay, especially when the cuddles are coupled with meaningful and truthful reviews of the joy you experienced during the sex. Something like a compliment, or a touch in an erogenous zone.

Sexual Mindfulness

In *Chapter 2* we asserted that sex happens in the mind. But our minds are such a complex part of our existence. I can be sitting next to my wife and my mind can be half-way around the world, where my favourite football team is playing. I remember a song that used to play where the singer complained that his partner's body was with him, but her mind was on the other side of town. It's a grievous experience, one that creeps up in many people's lives. Wives are often culpable in this area, as they are physiologically designed to have capacity for multiple brain activities at once. This is why my wife is better at multi-tasking than I am.

Some tips to improve mindfulness:

- Remove distractions

I find this to be quite helpful when I am working from home. There are so many other things you may consider doing other than the thing you want to do. Like getting to the gym and taking a thousand selfies before getting to the workout you were there to do. Or noticing that 35 minutes have gone by with you on your phone instead of typing out that report for work. Distractions are a reality in life generally, and even more a reality during sex. I find that removing the common culprits helps a lot, like turning off your cell phone or putting it on a setting that doesn't disturb you. Now some people may argue that this is bad advice because "what if you get a call that something happened to someone you love"? Let me give you a reality check- in the years since I have been married, I have received one call to an emergency. That's 4 years, and one call. If I had kept my cell phone on during this time, the distraction would not be a call, but the lack of a call that I expect because I am always thinking 'what if?' The lesson here is to switch off your phone, but more importantly, switch off your mind to the possibility of being called.

Other distractions include things like a squeaky bed. I've experienced one of those myself. I err on the side of a bit of OCD, so that really took the wind out of my sails (if you know what I mean). That was when we decided on a new bed. This was back when it was just the two of us. We had a situation with our headboard once, and it was quite unnerving because we had a guest. Try and plan yourself ahead of time when having guests, avoid doing stuff that will make you more self-conscious and less present in the moment.

- Don't overthink

The problem with advice like this is that you are told what not to do, and not what to do. As humans, we are wired to understand life in contrasts (mostly, that is). Good vs. Bad, Light vs. Dark, Love vs. Hate... So being told not to overthink elicits the question of 'What do I do instead?' or 'what is overthinking?' I don't have the liberty to detail what overthinking is in this, but simply; overthinking is investing more mental energy and attention to something than is needed. This usually takes the form of repetitive mulling over something even when you're supposed to be engaged in something else. In sex, this may be thinking about how badly you were the last time you tried a new sex position, and repeating that thought so much that it takes away focus from what is happening in the now.

- Let your talk, be sex talk (clean, adult talk) ...

One of the easiest things to do to increase your likelihood of being present and in the moment is talking through your thoughts. What are you feeling, what are you seeing, what are you loving about your spouse, what do you want to do to them, what is their action doing to you. All this, spoken with love and using appropriate language[22] is helpful, because if you have to vocalise your thoughts, they tend to be focused on what is happening. The merging of mental and vocal action calls for singular focus. It also tends to enhance the anticipation of the listening spouse, because being told what is about to happen weirdly plant imaginations on what that would feel like, etc... You obviously have to take turns talking, making sure that no one is overhearing you. A cute tip here is to whisper into each other's ears. The warmth of your breath and the contents of your words are likely to spice this action up. It doesn't have to be rigid, but you have to 'give-and-take', take turns. This way, it all becomes a dialogue and before you know it- you're comfortable talking during sex. For more on 'sex talk' see Chapter 7.

It may be a wonder to you why sex talk is so important. What makes it so important to talk during sex, isn't sex supposed to be a physical interaction, not verbal? Well, the answer is that the physical aspects of the engagement must be guided by verbal ques, if you were to have sex silently, how do you communicate? Do you make signs? Perhaps signs may work, but if you are capable of speaking, then do so. Football fans (or soccer for the American reader) will remember how games that were televised during COVID-19 lockdowns had sound edited to them to give them a real feel. Why? Because the experience is not complete when it is wordless. In conclusion- speak!!! If that doesn't do it, then you must remember that the creation of the world came about by the word... they are powerful, use that power.

Supplements

Sexual enhancing supplements are everywhere. You can visit any supermarket store; it is highly likely that you will find some product that promises performance in this area. This is where convenience is dangerous, because convenience today could cost your ability tomorrow (Viagra insert). It's like staking long term sustainability on short-term gains; you lose feeling like a winner. Sexual health begins with overall health and sexual dysfunctions are usually indicators of health issues- like heart disease, diabetes, etc... So don't paper over your struggles to 'get-it-up' by taking something. Using sexual drugs, your wife may hail you a sexual maverick, but the cost is too great. Whatever the issue, it's best to see a professional about it and treat the problem from the source. I say this with kindness and respect, but I am seeing the medical profession move ever so swiftly towards pharmacology, where a lot of ailments are being managed rather than cured, and the recommendation is often a pill and not a lifestyle change. So be careful.

For those who have no need for such supplements, keep it that way. My recommendation would be taking preventative measures while you have the chance; exercise[23], eat a healthy diet, drink plenty of water, sleep well and avoid habits that will result in health issues down the road. Another key ingredient is the avoidance of stress - sex and exercise both do well in reducing stress, but you're also less effective *in the sack* when you're taking on a lot of stress. Healthy relationships also help in avoiding stress, most times our relationships are the causes of stress. Work stress is also something to keep in check, I know this personally because I've worked in audit, and peak seasons usually signal a peak in stress levels and lower sex drive, if any.

It would be improper for me to shun supplements completely. Some supplements contribute to overall health, and by extension, improve our sexual health. These are not forbidden. For example, my wife felt constantly tired following the birth of our son, this was because of the toll that motherhood took on her while she had to juggle domestic life and a career. The nurse at the infant clinic recommended that she took multi-vitamin supplements to avoid being deficient in key macro and micronutrients. This was a huge revelation for me, more like an in-your-face discovery. As a breast-feeding mom, much of our son's nutrients came from her, so she was effectively powering two people, so a bit of help is never a problem. But as always, it is best to consult your healthcare professional before taking anything.

Your Sex Life

Your sex life is *your* sex life. It is yours to do with as you wish. In the same vein, it is yours to deal with when it isn't what you want. The idea that something is yours speaks to your ownership of it, and responsibility for it. When it goes in a direction that doesn't suit you, you have to look in the mirror. Unfortunately, looking at yourself in the mirror can be a little difficult to do in sex because it is a two-man job. This calls for communication, but what is communication?

One of the best definitions I have heard on what communication is, goes something like this, 'communication is transferring a message such that the receiver has the same understanding as the sender' In other words, communication is not just expressing something in words, but true communication is when the expression is interpreted by the received of the communication the same way that the sender intended and understands. So, for your sex life to become what you desire, the desires you have must become a shared desire. Anything less than is an indicator of a mismatch in your common understanding of what you want it to be. Sadly, this leads to a lot of conflict.

Fighting Fair

Conflict is usually a situation to avoid in any relationship, but conflict should be an area of relationship that we get comfortable with navigating through. The idea of conflict as something to navigate through is quite telling. It implies that conflict is unavoidable in relationship. Anyone who's been married long enough would agree to this; you don't always see eye-to-eye with your spouse. In fact, much of your disagreements are a matter of personality, preference or perspective. Individuality is the reason behind all this, but individuality is a tricky blessing to have. For one, it sets us apart from all other humans before or after us. But it also means that our views will be biased toward said individuality. This is when conflict arise.

I concede that our conflict can arise from various sources, but at the heart of it all is the differences borne out of our individuality. The key thing is understanding this as the source of conflict and recognising that our disagreements don't make us enemies, but they present an opportunity to reason with each other and grow together. In a sexual context, differences can take the form of favouring different positions, differences in our disposition to trying new things, frequency of sex due to our natural sex drives, and a host of other things. Sorting through and navigating these can be a challenge.

Differences in a sexual context are the cause of many a fight between couples, and the thing about fights is that the parties involved are always on a quest for 'blood'. It is never a case that an individual enters an argument or conflict with the view other than to win. By win, I mean prove that they are right and as a consequence, the other party is wrong. This is done at all costs. What I advocate for is approaching conflict with a questioning mind; ask yourself why your spouse so resistant on this matter? What is important to them that they'd go to such lengths to defend their positon? Usually, when you pursue understanding more than you do besting your spouse, you unlock empowering information that can lead to some of the most meaningful conversations.

Are you good in bed? *(Double entendre)*

The bedroom, and the bed are universally accepted as prime locations for sexual action. The phrase 'good in bed' or 'the sack' is unanimously accepted as a description of sexual prowess. It's no surprise then, that creating a great environment in the bedroom and investing in a quality bed are key ingredients of a great sex life. Sure, sex can and often does happen in other places, but more often than not - the bedroom and the bed are prime real estate... I remember when we had an old bed, let's just say the squeaks weren't necessarily musical when things got 'heated'. We'd often remark on how those squeaks would snitch on us when we have guests. A quality bed was one of the best investments ever, I mean we're talking about the spot where you spend much of your life. The recommend sleeping time is 6 - 8hours per night. If you sleep 7 hours a day, that's 49 hours a week. Over a year, that's 2548 hours a year. That's about 106 days, which is three-and-a-half months. All spent asleep. Add to that the hours of inexplicable sexual pleasure, a quality bed becomes a no brainier. Besides a bed, depending on what you fancy, there may be other items you make use of during sex. Prior preparation of these items is important in making sex pleasurable and hassle-free. Any discomfort in this area may become a deterrent that domino's into something much more problematic.

The other aspect of being good in bed is the small matter of answering whether you perform well in sex. The simple answer to this is that being good in bed is subjective and relative. Subjective, in that different people consider different things to be good in bed. Relative, because there's always a point of reference when measuring the success of anything. The best person to give us feedback on how well we're doing in bed is of course your spouse.

I was advised that my wife is the barometer for how well I am doing as a husband. She's the only person capable of reviewing my performance in marriage. However, her review of this and my performance in the sack will be biased because they will tend toward what she likes, and whether I give that to her. So that the real starting point in pursuing sexual prowess is discussing each other's preferences in sex and accepting that these will change over time. We should remember that sex is a journey and things change along the way, so it's always good to keep in check. But being great at sex is a matter of satisfying your spouse's desires. This is the complete opposite of what the world teaches about being good in bed, the content is mostly about the person who wants to be good, rather than the person you want to be good to or for.

A word for First timers

You may be starting your journey of sex and marriage or be at a point where you don't even remember your first time. We men are guilty of forgetting, but the women who have sex for the first time on their wedding nights remember the pain[24].

The anatomy of the female is fascinating, but I won't go into that here. But in a summative sense, the vaginas are elastic in nature, so they build a tolerance for the insertion of objects, such as the male penis. I say objects because some people use fingers and their mouth/tongue (more on this in Chapter 7). Building up this elasticity takes patience and time. Sex for the first time is usually painful for most women, because their private parts need to adjust to what is being put into them. It also follows that nervous energy tends to make us stiff, so when women approach their first time, they are usually nervous and that adds to the stiffness.

A few tips include taking your time with foreplay. Although caressing, kissing and stroking erogenous zones will be foreign in the initial stages, simply talking each other through the process and giving constant feedback is a great start. Make sure that you are both breathing and relaxed. Don't rush the point of insertion, I know it can be tempting because men get aroused much easier than the women. A great rule of thumb is to do so when you are both warmed up, which is usually indicated by the release of moistening fluids in your genitals. Once penetrated, use gentle strokes as you both acclimatise to the sensation. It may not last very long, and that is okay. Take breaks as necessary but keep the communication and feedback alive. Repeat this exercise until you both begin to get comfortable with each other and the idea of having sex. Remember that it is only enjoyed together, if one of you is hurting, you are both hurting.

Another mistake I made is avoiding sex because I thought it was hurting my wife. I know this sounds a little crazy, but power through the pain gently and patiently. Don't lose the willingness to keep trying. My other mistake was wanting to try too much too soon, just stick to one position, preferably the missionary (or man-on-top) position. This way you can maintain eye contact and the penetrating party has more control over the flow. Consider using a pillow to elevate the wife's behind.

The biggest cause of pain is being overly eager to penetrate while the wife is not mentally ready for this. Patience is key. I heard someone say that the speed during sex, especially during foreplay is slower than your definition of slow. Another cause for pain is friction. Friction is what takes place when an unaroused vagina is penetrated prematurely. Actually, friction can cause scarring for both husband and wife, which is not a great experience. To avoid this, try getting yourselves a lubricant[25] that is free of fragrances and the fixings they have out there. You can order this online if you fear being seen getting it over the counter. But buy some and use it, it will simulate the moisture and make your first experience less painful. With sex, the wetter the better. Lastly, if you plan to use any of these tips, be sure to talk it over with your spouse before trying it.

Now I know that I have given some descriptive content, but I feel that it is worth doing so in order to help avoid some mistakes from the beginning. It is amazing how your sex life can be made or broken by your initial experience. It's easy to see why. If I were to ask you the details around your trip to work or school a week or so ago, it may be difficult to remember. Especially if you have been there for a while, but if you are asked to talk about your first day there, you are more likely to remember details because everything was new to you then and your mind had not zoned you out to the less useful bits of information about your work environment. The same goes for our sex life, we are much more likely to remember our 1st time than our 100th time, unless you are a stats person. Some people have a dislike for sex because of a terrible experience on their first time, and a lack of improvement since. Don't be those people, I hope your reading this book is proof enough that you're not.

In conclusion, I think the overarching principle from this chapter should be the need for relational intimacy, and how this should always precede physical intimacy. When you prioritise getting to know your spouse; what they like, their dislikes, what they want, etc... becoming great at sex becomes easy- just do what he/she likes. In turn, seeing your spouse experience pleasure when you do what they like will bring your pleasure. Even more exciting is the fact that the whole deal is reciprocal, so when you focus of satisfying your spouse's needs, they tend to want to do the same for you. This focus on relational intimacy does not take away from the need to have healthy and able bodies for sex. Healthy, in the sense that sexual activity can be engaged in by both spouses without harm to their health. Able, in the sense that holding whatever sex position is not an out-of-reach feat that only Olympians can do. All this is possible by taking care of our bodies, and this concept is littered across this text.

Chapter 6: Your Sexual History

People say history repeats itself. Some say a lot can be learnt from our history. I say history can teach us many lessons, but we can also empower it to debilitate us. In a sense, I do agree with the assertion that history repeats itself, but only if we allow it to.

An undealt-with past (your history), has a way of chaining you if you allow it. But confronting it, and dealing with it, especially with what the Word of God says, usually brings a newness never-before seen.

Past, Present, Future

- Our past shapes the way we view life and the future. Ask any psychologist/therapist, most of our issues in adult life are a result of complexes built from our past experiences. The challenge is that many of us do not realise this until it's too late. Whether the past experiences are our fault or the fault of others, it affects us either way.

I was listening to one of Myron Golden's teachings on YouTube, and he said past perceived voids create present pursued values. What he meant by this is that what we have seen as lacking in our life in the past, usually informs what we value in the future. In my case, for a long time in my childhood, we never had a car in my family. In a South African context, this was quite inconvenient because our public transportation system is not famed for its efficiency. So as an adult, I value owning a vehicle of my own. This is so valuable for me because it's something I lacked in the past. This goes even further, because I always wished my parents would drop me off at school like the other kids, but this never happened. In my case, I want to be able to provide that comfort for my children.

My vehicle story is a mild example of how the past can and usually does affect our future, it could be worse. For example, being sexually violated by someone in your childhood. The truth is that some of the things in our past were not a result of things we could control. However, we let our undealt-with pasts hinder our future by living life in the 'here-and-now' through the lens of yesterday's struggles.

I suppose this is the key discussion to have during courtship, getting into your partner's past and try to understand what contributed to the person who now sits in front of you. In my marriage, we spent three-and-a-half years getting to know each other closely before we got married. This was not planned, because I wanted to get married the moment she said yes. But in hindsight, I realise what a blessing that time was in solidifying our relationship and where we wanted to go as a couple. Over the period of our courtship, a lot came up from our past that shaped the way we interacted with each other and our understanding of ourselves intra-personally.

In my case, I struggled with the sense of abandonment, especially from a female, namely, my mom. I felt that she left me quite early on in life and that her limited involvement in my life was tied to my decision to choose my father over her in the 'custody battle'. I've since had some talks with her, but a residue of the past pain still comes up to date. How does this affect my sex life? Easily, I struggle with rejection. Being rejected in my sexual advances strikes that nerve emotionally, in fact rejection coming from a loved one is usually met with very high walls of self-preservation. I won't delve into my story, but I hope that the glimpse I have given you is sufficient to illustrate the point.

In dealing with the issue of my past, my wife and I had several conversations as a couple where she reassured me that she was not planning on 'jumping ship' anytime soon. She was here to stay.

Not only was there a conversation, but substantiating action to reassure me that she was not leaving. My fear of abandonment was so real that I often folded in arguments because in my mind an argument would likely result in a split and I would be 'divorced' before I even got to be married, and the fact that I would have yet another woman exit the door of my life. This past experience required much praying and counselling, plus the supportive reassurance of my wife.[26]

Moving on with life from this past hurt, I am constantly aware of the enemy's intention to use my past to cripple me in the future. We must not forget that the enemy, Satan, is a trickster. One of his favourite tricks is to use our past to instil fear in us. How many people are out there saying 'men are trash' and that men should not be trusted? These are the same people who enter into relationships with their guard on high alert because they expect their husbands to hurt them the same way that they've been hurt before or seen others get hurt. This is the enemy's trick; to steal your joy, kill your confidence in your marriage (or your spouse) and destroy all hope of a successful marriage. Fear and doubt are his biggest weapons.

- Fear is the consciousness of danger/harm when there is no basis for it. This is usually the result of previous experiences. These play into our marriages as they determine what we expect out of our sexual relationships. If you have a fear that your spouse will leave you, the tendency will be to reserve a piece of yourself just so your spouse doesn't take all of you when they *eventually leave*. This could include your sexual relationship, as you hold back during sex for the same reasons. Another manifestation of fear is one I am too familiar with, rejection. Being the child of divorcees, I grew up with the sense that my mom abandoned me as a child, so I had to realise how this held me back in my marriage, as I avoided making sexual advances at times because I feared the feeling of rejection.

There are many other ways our past hurts and the fears that they've created can debilitate us, key to winning against these limitations is the realisation that they are limitations. Then taking steps to rewire our minds to the reality of our current relationships and possibly the safety that our spouse assures. This is definitely one for discussion among married couples, as your spouse can help positively reinforce the truth that your current situation no longer warrants the fears you once held. All you need to do is understand that the two of you are a team and that you can help each other rewire your internal system such that happiness and stability in relationship is a norm, not a 'relationship goal'.

My wife comes from a background where faithfulness among married men is non-existent. She also grew up with a father who was a heavy alcoholic. So, I took the decision that I would never drink alcohol, not even on occasion. This was because I never wanted her to have flashbacks of her father in me, even though she never asked me to do that. I wanted to remove all possibilities of doubt and/or fear that I was becoming something that traumatised her as a child. I also committed myself to faithfulness in my marriage, to avoid her having any reason to believe the narrative she grew up being fed about men. You see, I am from the Zulu tribe, she's from the Xhosa tribe. The narrative where's she's from was that Zulu men are physically abusive cheaters. This was all the motivation I needed, and I will pursue dispelling these false beliefs till the day I die. Your spouse may have had different experiences in the past, with impacts great and small. Are you aware of these? If not, why? If you're aware, what have you committed yourself to doing to protect them from ever feeling like their reliving that past? Take initiative and have the conversation on your own fears and/doubts. Realise that you disempower these things when you speak about them.

Lean into your fantasies and fetishes

In chapter 4, we touched on BDSM, and it often indicating a deeper issue, usually from the past. This, along with having absurd fetishes is often a result of an undealt-with past. No one in their right mind would want to humiliate another, more so their spouse. The word refers to a married couple as one flesh, why would I want to humiliate myself?[27]

Our likes and dislikes are often pointed in the direction of our past. One unrelated, but relevant example is my wife's strong dislike for maize porridge. Most African people would be familiar with this dish, it's a staple breakfast in South Africa, especially in formerly rural areas. The history of this dish is that my wife was fed porridge as a child under less than pretty circumstances. So, she has a bit of a traumatic history associated with eating porridge. It is so bad that she despises it and a few spoonsful of it are enough to send her gagging to the bathroom. The surprising thing is that shortly after giving birth to our son, she had a few days where she struggled with producing breastmilk as her body adjusted to having given birth. My mom recommended that she eats maize porridge as it is known to encourage milk supply... to say she was eating porridge with vigour doesn't begin to explain what happened. We were all excited to finally share the dish with her. Thankfully, her milk supply came in on the 4th day post-partum, and oh the joy. Remarkably, the desire for maize porridge fizzled and we were back to the gag-reflexes. What we can learn from this observation is that our desires and dislikes can be traced to our past.

Dislikes are often linked to traumas, while desires take us back to happy times. Traumas can also inspire desires, especially if they recreate a traumatic scenario, we experienced but we're in an elevated role of control, either consciously or sub-consciously. An example of this is men who want to be dominant as a means of validating their manhood in response to being molested. These are examples of some vile behaviours in response to undealt-with traumas from our past.

Though this isn't a fetish, but I once heard a story of a couple who were on the brink of separation because the lady felt like her husband did not love her enough. Upon further interrogation by the counsellor, it was discovered that the root of her feeling 'unloved' was the fact that the husband did not physically assault her. This emanated from her previous relationships which led her to falsely associate physical assault with being loved. It is weird, and may sound crazy, but people go through these things. It is the same reason why men who grew up in homes where their fathers abused their mothers tend to become abusers themselves. Somehow, the psychology is that being abusive is the correct behaviour, or in serious cases, the abuse they perpetrate on their wives is a warped form of justice for their mothers. If any of this plagues you, my advice is that you seek out a reputable Christian counsellor or psychologist who will help you deal with your past. Even if all seems well, seeking reputable, professional help can be instrumental in identifying blind spots or even casting out doubts.

Another aspect of fantasies and fetishes is the lack thereof. Sometimes we do not struggle from a lack of desire, or imagination but we struggle for the fact that we do not allow ourselves to desire or imagine. We've all been created in the image of God, and in this way, we are all capable of desire and imagination- lean into this power you have been given by God, and let nothing stop you from desiring the things that God has in store for you concerning your marriage, even in the realm of sex. Don't be afraid to try that new position you read about in Chapter 3, or something you felt inspired to try but held back for fear of being ridiculed. Commit to being an open book to your spouse, and to being free to express all your desires to each other.

Speaking of desires, the Word of God instructs us to delight ourselves in the Lord, and He will give us the desires of our hearts. Explaining this scripture, a gentleman once alluded to the fact that delighting in the Lord requires yielding to His Word. Inadvertently, this aligns us with desiring what *He desires*, so that in the end, when we delight in Him, He gives us the desires of His heart[28]. What this means for us in any area of life, including sex within our marriage, is that when we yield it to God, along with ourselves, our desires become His desires, and His desires and ways are much higher than our thoughts and fantasies can perceive.

Social Media

It is difficult to write anything these days without giving social media the nod. It has permeated society and become so interwoven with our lives that it is difficult to estimate its reach. Much of the views that people hold about anything; climate change, governance and politics, pop culture, etc... all of these are in some way influenced by social media. The harshness of social media is that it never forgets and you're always at risk of getting cancelled. Since much of our lives are available for consumption on social media, it is difficult to erase what you have done and posted on social media. You may remove it from your profile, but those who know will forever know.

There are some who are victims of the unforgiving nature of social media. Perhaps you have had your body be the subject of discussion on social media, for whatever reason. You may have been intentional in instigating this, but you did not know better. How do you deal with this? You may have even been the subject of a sexual video, and wonder how your spouse will live with this? These are all matters that have become a reality because of the power of social media. Social media may also be the lens through which you view what the ideal body type is, and your body seems to be anything but. I have a word of encouragement for you.

We were created in the image of God that is our beings are radiant reflections of who He is. Regardless of your body type, if you take care of it as you should, i.e., eat healthily, drink water and avoid consuming anything toxic, your body will reciprocate this by being healthy. If you feel that you are too fat, then do something about the excess weight- wallowing in self-pity will do you no good. Take action. If your concerns are relating to things you cannot change, then it may be a good idea to embrace these features about yourself and appreciate them for what they are. Sure, you can get surgery for some things, but the surgery will not purge your insecurity. Instead, it will inflate your ego because of something that isn't truly yours. As for being made in the image of God, your body is not the image of God, your spirit (inner man) is.

The other word of encouragement is aimed at our need to regulate what catches our attention. Too much time is spent on social media under the pretence of connecting with the world when all we are doing is disengaging from the reality of our lives. This is a milestone on the road to depression.

Take charge, and gain control over how you spend your time. Remembering that doubt is created in the eyes, so what you see on your phone or TV is usually what contributes to negative self-talk and negative feelings of comparing ourselves to others.

If you have been the subject of sexual content on social media, realise that you are a new creation in Christ. Sure, the old has passed away but the memories that people have of you haven't. The enemy will use this as a tool to derail you from your faith journey. In my experience, what we admit to, and embrace loses its foothold on us, this is why confession is so powerful. In the case of a past experience that is known to many and is typically a cause for shame, own up to it. This way, no one can use it against you, rather, it becomes an example of hope for some who are still stuck where you have been. Don't let the devil use your past to hold you down. Let God use your past for advancing His Kingdom and let him raise an army from the dry bones of your messy past.

Finally in this segment, make use of social media for good. You may read the above and think I have issues against it. On the contrary, I believe social media is a great place for connecting with people and positively impacting the life of others. The key is to use it responsibly and conduct yourself as you would with live people around you.

Body Image

Body image impacts our confidence in the sack. This is our perception of our own bodies. An example, people who have larger frames tend to be self-conscious about the way they look. I know someone who doesn't eat in public for fear of being judged because she is a 'big person'. What this person's belief means is that they do not deserve to eat in public because they are too fat. No one has said anything to her to that effect, but her own beliefs have limited the places she can enjoy a meal, even if it is "healthy". There are various sources of issues with body image, which contribute negatively to our confidence in sex.

- **Weight**

The most gruesome prisons are not maximum-security incarceration centres, but the prisons we subject ourselves to in our minds. When we believe that we are unworthy, we behave like we are, and we speak like we are. In a sexual context, this takes the form of not believing you're worthy of sexual attention because you are a certain weight. Even when your spouse reassures you that you are wonderful and that they are attracted to you, you cast this aside and hold fast to you false confessions. Much of these are born out of our own actions, as our bodies often reflect our dietary and exercise habits. Sadly, people who are insecure about their bodies on account of weight rarely do anything to change it, but wallow in self-pity by eating themselves to illness. Believer, beware!!! Don't fall into gluttony. If you are uncomfortable with your body mass, you have the power to change it by changing your habits. Take care that this desire does not become a stronghold.

- **Ageing**

The other source of body image issue is ageing. Ageing is the natural process of growing. I always held the conviction that the phenomenon of becoming weaker as you age is God's way of reminding us to rely on His strength, not our own... Popular culture tends to frown upon ageing. From celebrity surgeons to high-end cosmetics, much is done to slow down or even reverse this process... Self-doubt = fear, perfect love casts out fear.

- **Naked and unashamed**

Shame is the result of our past experiences where our worth was pit into question. A typical cause of such is when our body has been criticised because it differs in some way to that which is 'normal'. From the size of your genitals, your breasts being too small, your butt being too big, or some other feature which was used as an object for teasing... Most of the teasing and bullying causes us to feel we're less than we should be. So, nakedness is a very vulnerable state which is part of our sexual experience in marriage. We ought to trust that our spouse will love us despite our 'self-perceived' imperfections and in spite of the negative affirmations we've been told our whole lives concerning these. All of this plays into our sexual history, though not relating to sexuality. Their overall contribution to our appearance (which is fundamental to attraction) is what holds us back.

- **Surgery**

The availability of surgery has made changing parts of our bodies a very real possibility. Physical alterations are no longer a dream. At the right price, with the right expertise... You can become who you want to be, at least in a physiological sense. But the real you lives inside this 'mud hut' we call our body. Regardless of how many changes we make, what we ought to heal is the inner man. This is why so many people get multiple surgeries to alter their bodies. Because one simply isn't enough.

- **Negative feedback**

Sometimes the image our spouses have of themselves are borne out of the things we say about their bodies. You used to be a hunk, or you used to have such a figure... All this implies that they no longer do, and you appreciated that version of them better than you do the one they are now. My bishop, when he officiated our marriage said I should love my wife even when she becomes rounder. Funny I know, but funnier in my language. It is also deceptively profound. Why? Because our bodies change as we age, as we go through various stages of our lives. You may have been slim, like me because you were underweight and not eating as you should. In my case, it wasn't a lack of food but a lack of knowledge... Stop being critical of your spouse and appreciate them. I'd rather live peacefully with a wife who's slightly overweight and know that she respects me, loves me and is kind to me. Worse, she's that way temporarily because she just had a baby (in my case).

The image we have of what a woman should be must never be driven by pop culture. Define your own sexy and if your *sexy* is slim and toned, then try some other method of communicating that rather than nagging and criticising. My wife told me a story of how this man got his wife to exercise and lose weight. Realising that his wife was falling off the wagon of taking care of herself, and dragging him with, he spoke to his wife (I imagine this was done while seated and with love), asked her to help him get control of his weight. Told her he wanted to start walking and eventually jogging regularly in the mornings. He then kindly asked that she support him and join him because he knew that having a buddy will make him more accountable and encourage him to be consistent. What happened? They stuck to it and the wife lost the weight and so did he.

Insecurity

Shame is the reactive feeling of guilt. Guilt because you did stuff you shouldn't have. The interesting thing is that you had no idea how wrong these were at the time of commission. Jesus understood that people are capable of committing sins because they do not know better (see Luke 23:34)[29]. Shame is the feeling we have because of past actions; insecurity is the attitude we have following our shame. Insecurity is defined as "anxiety about oneself, or a lack of confidence" (Oxford Dictionaries, 2023). Anxiety about ourselves is basically a mismatch of identity. I wrote a book once, that has not been published yet and one of the things I write about is the identity crisis we face in society today. We are generally unaware of who we are, and therefore do not operate according to who we should be. In the context of our marriage, we become insecure when we have no confidence in who we are intrinsically (spiritually), we lack confidence in our appearance being attractive to our spouses (physically) and therefore our attitudes reflect one who is not loved and desired (mind). Ironically, insecure is the opposite of secure, which means stable. So that a person who is insecure is effectively unstable.

Lack of confidence in who we are intrinsically is down to our fallen nature, and the world and Satan constantly reaffirming the lie of our inadequacy. Perhaps you have experience in this in your past, where you were told, you would not amount to anything, or treated like a Cinderella. All this builds up the evidence that you are less than who you truly are. Over time, you begin to operate as though this were the truth. I believe that confidence in your being created in the image of God and what that means about your being on a spiritual level is the starting point of unlimited power in one's life. This is the objective of grace; repositioning man for purpose regardless of what he deserves.

What often keeps people from attaining this grace is the idea that they do not deserve it. Truly speaking, you don't deserve it, but the sacrifice of Jesus Christ has made you deserving, because it is all grace. So, step out of your past and embrace the new life you have in Christ. Walk with confidence in that you are created in the image of God, have confidence in that you are attractive and are deserving of love because Christ made you so. I promise you, when you adopt this attitude, you will be sexier and more attractive to your spouse.

Consider this, the scripture says "... *A nagging wife is like water going drip-drip-drip.* (Proverbs 19:13 GNB)". It does not say an ugly wife, or a wife that is unpleasant to the eyes. Which means that the cause of a woman being insufferable and unbearable to live with has nothing to do with appearance, but her attitude. This is because a nagging person is nothing but someone who lacks an attitude of gratitude. In fact, some versions refer to the nagging as quarrelling, which is to brawl or fight. This is likened to water going drip-drip-drip in the GNB. To give you an illustration of how devastating the scenario referred to in this scripture, there is something called the Chinese Water Torture. In this method of torture, the victim is bound, and water is dripped onto their heads at irregular intervals. The effect is not to get information, but to induce anxiety, psychosis and the loss of touch with reality. I dare say that some men have gone through and continue to go through all three because of a nagging wife. All this makes the man insecure, and the same effect is possible for wives when the husband engages in nagging too. Both spouses need to mind their tongue, and work on creating an environment of safety around each other. Your spouse should never feel less than secure (i.e., insecure) around you, he/she should be free to be *naked and unashamed* when you're around (figuratively, literally and euphemistically, depending on context).

Family

A lot of what we think about sex is formed by the conversations we've had in our family. The existence of a narrative on sex shapes our views on sex. In equal manner, the non-existence of a narrative opens us up to apprehension when sex is being discussed or worse, pop culture's whims and woes.

A great part of who we are as people is formed by the experiences, we have had in our family lives. If your upbringing is anything like mine, you would identify with what it means to eat, sleep, and breathe the faith. I was raised in a faith-based home, and I do not remember having a single conversation about sex with any of my parents. Even the one reference to sex was a prohibition from having babies before wedlock. It would be reasonable to think that my view of sex was from the perspective of how not to do it. The problem with a mind-set focused on what not to do, it disregards context and disregards *what to do*. Which is why some people struggle with the concept of sex when they enter into marriage, because they have conditioned their minds to the idea that sex = bad. Having gone through a large chunk of your conscious experience believing this, it takes more than a night to accept the truth that 'sex with my wife/husband = **good**'. Just remember this, the power is knowing and applying this truth by reframing your mind (more on this later).

To parents, and those planning to be parents; please take note of the narratives you perpetuate in your family. Be mindful of the seeds being sown into your children because they can make or break them in future. I recently saw a documentary where the public is invited to attend group therapy with inmates of a maximum-security prison. From this, I realised the power of a parent, especially fathers. To say the role parents play in children's lives is important is an understatement.

The Trump Card for Your Past

One of the cornerstones of Christian salvation is the grace of God through Christ. Grace is often referred to as *Unmerited Favour*. I like to look at it as *favour regardless of merits* because the entire doctrine of grace elevates us from the lows of what we have done. We are forgiven all our sins, including sexual sin. It is also the responsibility of other believers to echo the newness of life in Christ (see 2 Corinthians 5:17). The problem is that the effects of our past actions are not wiped away. A baby out of wedlock is a reminder of actions past, possibly even a link to a previous toxic relationship. There is healing in Christ. There is hope in Jesus, and that hope is that Jesus is our Redeemer.

Redemption is the idea that something or someone is saved from something, or that something or someone has their faults paid for. There's a deeper theological study on how Jesus' death and resurrection does both to appease God's requirements for our sin and to save us from it. Allow me to take a different viewpoint on redemption.

As a person trained in commerce, my worldview is impacted by such training and in the world of commerce, redemption carries a different meaning. When something is redeemed, its value is realised. For example, when a cheque is cashed-in, the value to which the holder of such cheque is realised. In my view, this says to me that our past lives in sin are an undervaluation of who and what we are. We were made in the image of God, but all this value is undermined (excuse the pun) by the oppression of sin, even sexual sin. But in Christ, the true value of who and what we are is realised day-by-day so that we are becoming like Him. This is the Good News, the fact that by Christ's sacrifice we are redeemed. But there is a subtle tactic of the enemy that gives our past a foothold on our *NOW.*

The comparison conundrum

Comparison is one of the ways that we subtly give power to our past. The funny thing about this is that we don't realise that we are empowering our past. We always view life from two perspectives: absolutes and relatives. Absolutes are unchanging ideals such as the Truth of God's word. Relatives are where we trip up, we compare one experience against another rather than enjoying it for what it is. The subtlety is in the fact that we compare our life to what it was, and we base our enjoyment of our now on how it differs from our past. We have to get to a point where we enjoy our current life for what it is and only what it is, that is true contentment.

What this looks like in sex in a marriage context is this- we always compare how good things are versus how bad they were. What we don't realise is that by comparison, we are flashing back to the things that were and considering them in the context of the *Now.* A practical example is a spouse that it thankful of how The Lord has changed their life and moves to 'appreciate' how their life is 'so much better' than it was. What tends to happen thereafter is a trip down memory lane that gives importance to the past. It does this by rating the goodness of the *NOW* in the context of the badness of the *then.* It is not wrong to acknowledge the past, nor is it wrong to celebrate your progress since then. The issue is celebrating the *NOW* through the lens of your past. A simple shift of the mind in this area is likely to reframe your perspective.

Speaking of reframing perspective and shifting the mind, the Scriptures exhort us to the renewal of our minds (see Romans 12:2). The renewal of our minds does not involve unlearning so much as it requires new learning. Most times when we are encouraged to step out of the imprisonment of our past, we are told that there are things we need to unlearn for change to come. I submit to you that learning intrinsically involves 'unlearning'. That is to say what we learn and accept as truth forces out the lies that we may have accepted as truth before. The question is how do we learn these truths? And how do we begin to shift our minds towards such truths...? The answer lies in the pages of the Bible. The scriptures say

"Finally, brothers, whatever is true, whatever is honourable, whatever is just, whatever is pure, whatever is lovely, whatever is commendable, if there is any excellence, if there is anything worthy of praise, **think about these things**. What you have learned and received and heard and seen in me—practice these things, and the God of **peace** will be with you (Philippians 4:8-9 ESV)."

From the above passage we see that we have been given guidance on what to think. We have also been given the consequences of thinking this way, which is the God of peace being with us. I love this part particularly because of what peace means in the context of our past. First, let us agree that having the God of Peace with you is as good as having peace with you, the two are inseparable. What is peace? The word used here is "eirēne" which means rest, to join and 'set at one again' (Strong, 1890). This, peace brings rest as makes us whole again. As followers of Christ, we have access to this peace by Him who loved us, this peace can bring wholeness in the areas where we have been broken through past experiences. It can bring rest from the burdens that have beset us up to this point.

Finally, it may occur to you that we have dealt largely with our past in the context of sexual matters. It is important that I zoom into sexual history in the context of this book. However, your sexual history is a part of your history, and our history affects the way we approach our present and the future. Where your history is plaguing your marriage, resolve to deal with it hand-in-hand with your spouse.

Chapter 7: Oral Sex

Oral *adjective*

/ˈɔːrəl/

/ˈɔːrəl/

[1] [usually before noun] spoken rather than written

[2] [only before noun] connected with the mouth

Using our mouths

For many virgin Christians, the idea of oral sex irks them, especially the women. For some, it is scary- the thought of having their future husband put their penis into their vulva (vagina) is terrifying when some women don't want so much as a tampon stuck in there. For guys, like me, the anxiety kicks in when you think about the statistics of men's longevity during sex and how this compares to women. My heart used to race each time I thought of this, I often wondered if I'd ever be enough... silently. Now adding the image of having your spouse's genitals in your mouth to the already daunting task of sex is just horribly terrifying.

Many couples would be years into their marriage without ever experiencing oral sex. In some marriages, it is one-sided because the other is either ashamed to have their spouse go down south, or the non-participating spouse is grossed out. Either way, if you don't have oral sex as part of your arsenal then you're missing out.[30]

The other aspect of sex is the first iteration of the definition of oral sex, as shown above. Specifically, the verbal element. Sex is an issue of the mind and one of the apparatuses requires use of oral means for it to succeed. What you do or do not say could determine how great your sex life is.

Below are some common issues with oral sex & key points of advice should you have an interest in trying it or want to enhance your experience in this area.

- **Hygiene**[31] (*and the lack thereof*) is usually the chief culprit in people's aversion to oral sex.

For example, when women use the bathroom to pass fluids, pubic hairs can be a nightmare because they tend to hold the urine odour down there. So that skipping a shower may be a turn-off for your spouse. Sex juices themselves can be a turn-off when another round is considered. The solution to all this is to adopt better hygiene habits. It must be noted that I am not advocating for the removal of pubic hairs, they wouldn't be there if they served no function. In fact, I would advise husbands this way; if your lady is comfortable keeping them, embrace it. Otherwise, the below are bound to keep things fresh, so let's discuss them:

- **Taking a shower/bath at least once a day** is a good way to maintain hygiene. It is also a habit you can stack other good habits onto (Clear, 2018)[32]. This includes adding the habit of brushing your teeth (and tongue) before/after each wash (more on this below). I personally added push-ups to my hygiene habits for a while; this had my wife swooning each time I went shirtless. By shower, I mean washing your entire body. I live in Durban, which is a coastal city with tropical tendencies, so I shower twice a day. Ladies, you may consider using a feminine wash down there if you are prone to odour. Something that is good on your skin and balances the pH *down there*. Be careful of products that are fragranced as they may change the natural order of things. Drinking more water is also a great way to deal with vaginal odour, much of body odour is down to our bodies trying to get rid of waste, and water is a great means of diluting and pushing this out.

- **Cutting and filing your nails regularly is super important**. Especially for men who like to use their fingers during foreplay. I've gone in with long nails before, and let's just say it wasn't pretty. The moaning that resulted was not the kind I wanted. I count that as a lesson learnt; **keep 'em short.**

- **Grooming**: cutting your hair, keeping it smelling clean, shaving, putting lotion over your skin to keep it hydrated because you don't want cracking heels and elbows scraping your sheets, or worse, your spouse. There are different opinions about shaving 'down there' my suggestion is to have the discussion with your spouse, let them guide you on what to do. As stated, be cautious to note that your pubic hairs serve a purpose of warding off infections, but they also retain that pee smell in women.

- **Doing laundry regularly**, especially bed linen and clothing. Nothing screams 'turn-off' than a pyjama that stinks. I advise investing in enough sleepwear to last you two weeks without doing laundry. This is a good metric, because it allows you to go that long without running out, but if you do laundry often, you will cycle these clothes well enough to prolong their life span. Changing sheets weekly is also a neat standard, so that you wash them with your weekly laundry. Nothing fires one up for sex than a clean, crisp set of bed linen. You can do it more often, depending on preference. The sniff test always works, but why wait for things to stink before changing? Why not use the power of technology and set a weekly reminder on your smart device, that way you're always on top of things #wink.

- I'm a strong proponent of **taking two showers and brushing your teeth and tongue twice a day**. Nothing takes the juice out of a whispered "I love you" than that onion breath or last night's meaty dinner. It's a turn off. Adopting a routine of brushing your teeth and tongue. Nothing more off-putting than a person who reeks of cologne and has a foul smell accompanying their every word. Remember that your diet also contributes to the state of your breath, so you might want to switch up your game to keep things fresh, and no, mints don't solve the issue, they paper over it. If you don't believe me, try eating a salad with raw onions and see how your kisses will be received by your spouse. I also advocate for visiting the dentist for a clean 1-2 times a year. This is not whitening, but a clean that will remove plaque build-up from your teeth. This is something I live by myself, in fact I live by much of what I advise others to do, and I figure it is only moral that one practices what they preach. Another habit I have built up (recommended by my dentist) is to invest in an aqua flosser. This is a devise that jets water into your mouth like a pressure washer, only small enough for it to be practical for oral use. I've found that the problem with building a habit of flossing is that it takes time. But with this device, I can do just as well as flossing in less than half the time. You can do your own reading on this, but our oral health contributes to our overall health.

- **Misconception of what sex and oral sex is** (*Christians and their missionary ways*)

- The history of the missionary position is muddied with misconceptions of sex. Like the one that the man would be on top because semen followed gravity and having the woman under would increase the likelihood of conception (see chapter 3). All this indicates to us is that the Christian's mind-set about sex is solely based on procreation and fulfilling God's command that we ought to be fruitful, multiply and subdue the earth. Though this is true, this is not the only reason for sex. In fact, if we believe this false notion about sex then there is no room for oral sex.

- Oral sex is a great way to get things heated between you and your spouse. But oral sex can just as well be the 'main event'. It is possible for one spouse to 'oralise' the other and things end there. When a husband *goes down on his wife* and pursues nothing further, this is like delaying the fun for the next sexual encounter (which may or may not involve penetrative sex). The point is **don't limit oral sex to foreplay only.**

- Biting! Oh! That is the nastiest thing that can happen during oral sex. Although people in secular circles like to call it 'eating him/her out', there is no chewing involved. Gentle does it, and like with other sexual acts, be willing to be guided by your spouse on what works for them. Partner with him/her in discovering this together and remember that the first time is always awkward.

- **Selfishness** (men wanting to be oralised but never returning the favour)

Men who have experience in the area of oral sex will tell you that the 'juices' down there are an acquired taste. But those who have an aversion to it are usually holding that positon because of a fear of being emasculated, or a fear of feeling less than. Like most fears, neither of these fears have a base. A man can never be emasculated by giving his wife pleasure. In fact, the ability to pleasure your wife does the opposite of emasculation. This in turn brings a sense of confidence and pride in the man, as he is able to give things to his wife no one else can.

- **Body Image issues** (women not wanting to go down on their men or being eaten out)

How we see ourselves affects how we interact with the world around us. It limits our potential and determines our parameters. In sex, our image of ourselves is usually referred to as our body image. This does not include our personality, which is an intangible. Our body image is our own perception of our body. Now our problem is that we chastise ourselves because our bodies aren't what **we think they should be.** This is all too common with the women; they fixate on being slimmer or toning this and that....

Sadly, many such women are in a cyclical process that stagnates their lives and worsens them; they pine over how fat or inadequate their bodies are compared to what they think they should be but do nothing to change that. Further, they adopt more of the habits that result in them worsening. I've seen this a lot with women in my circle; they complain about their need to lose weight and tone down, yet they go in strong in eating all the stuff that put them in that position. Unfortunately, nothing changes when you don't change. If you want to lose weight, you have to do and become what a person who weighs less is. Typically, this implies eating less and becoming more active. Stop complaining about things you're not willing to change. Otherwise, just accept these things because the laws of nature are such that who you are is the result of your thinking and the resulting actions done **consistently**. This is why the Scripture says, "Faith without works is dead". If you believe (faith) you should look different in a way that is possible through your actions, you should act (works) in a way that is consistent with your beliefs.

The other very important aspect of body image is the intangible, invisible self. This is the space where the things we cannot change about ourselves have been weaponised to make us feel less than. Much of these 'deficiencies' cannot be changed realistically. For example, the size of your head would be very difficult to change. Even when people lose a drastic amount of weight, their heads stay pretty much the same. Your height is also one of these things. Sometimes, the stuff we can change can also feel irreparable, like having a lot of weight, or other physical features that become the subject of shaming when we grow up. These leave a lasting mark on our inner person and affect the way we view ourselves and our behaviours. I was always teased about the size of my head growing up, was teased for many things, some not even physical. Just recently, I realised how deep my cousin's constant remarks of how awful I was at playing football went. I spent my entire life with an aversion to playing football. I even felt under pressure when I dared to play the game. In time, this morphed into a desire to play the game to prove to myself that I could do it despite the view that I was terrible at it. All of this was reactive, until I realised that my passions lie elsewhere and that I did not want to live my life reactively; trying to prove to myself that other people's opinions of me were wrong. This is how far-reaching words can be on our view of self.

- **Anal, manual stimulation and other 'out there' sexual practices-** *my views*

- I don't think any doctor or medical practitioner would consent to their patients ingesting faecal matter. I know this is a disgusting proposition for some, but there are some who may have heard of the concept of rimming (a.k.a. analingus). Which involves 'stimulating' the anus with the mouth/tongue. There are bacteria present in our waste that can cause illness and even death. Regardless of the precautions out there, it is too great a risk to try these acts. However, in respecting your choices, it is up to the couple to decide what they do with each other.

- Manual stimulation relates to the use of your fingers and hands to stimulate each other. What is colloquially referred to as a *hand-job*. This introduces some level of friction. Now friction, is the enemy of pleasure, unless a few rules are observed. First, never apply too much pressure, but let your spouse be your guide in terms of intensity and pressure. Especially in the initial stages of manual stimulation. This will avoid you hurting them, and nothing stings more than hurting the one you love when you had good intentions. Second, consider the use of a lubricant of your choosing. My recommendation is a silicone-based option that caters for sensitive skin. Try to avoid the scented kinds as the smell can get dizzying after some time. Otherwise, get creative in pleasuring each other with your hands if you are so inclined. You can use this as foreplay or use it as the 'main event', the choice is yours but there is pleasure to be had with your hands.

- One of the 'out there' practices I have seen is that of role-playing. Anyone who has had exposure to sexual literature of any nature would be familiar with the concept of the woman dressing up as a nurse and the husband playing the part of the patient. This is what role-playing is. It is using a particular narrative, like the patient-nurse one above, and adding a sexual dimension to it. This is arousing and enticing because it fuses playfulness and adventure of not knowing what comes next. Using our example above, the nurse can apply some 'ointment' to her wounded patient and *gently stroke* him to '*recovery*'. Or she can provide him with some '*stimulating medical applications*' to brighten his day. I will admit to being relatively inexperienced in this area, but it is an area of exploration for some. My advice is to avoid trying it too soon after marriage, just the basics of sex are enough to keep you occupied until role-playing becomes a factor. You don't want to enter such a practice while being a novice at the basic ins-and-outs of sex #wink.

Sex Talk – *the other form of oral sex*

One of the most powerful weapons both spiritually and emotionally is our tongue. The above portion of the book can be used to make a strong case for the physical power of the tongue (and mouth). But the tongue is more powerful in its spiritual and soul-based effects; that is a fact. However, many couples fail to make use of this power during sex by going through the entire sexual experience wordlessly. Men, we are usual culprits on this, we're all about business and we're so *in our heads* that we forget to communicate during sex. Below are some of the ways we can leverage the power of the tongue before, during and after sex:

- **Feedback**- what hurts, what's nice, what do you want. What are you feeling, what are you seeing, what are you loving about your spouse, what do you want to do to them, what is their action doing to you. (Chapter 5). In chapter 5 we spoke a bit about talking through your thoughts during sex. This is one simple trick to start you off on sex talk. In fact, this is all there is to sex talk, letting your spouse know what is happening in your mind concerning what is happening outside of it. When we simplify it like this, it seems less like rocket science and more like something that even the simplest people can do.

- **Endearment and encouragement-** *don't make me guess.*

My wife and I had an argument just recently. She had been looking at vacant land for something we had spoken about ages ago. So, on a ride home from getting a gas refill for the heater, out came the conversation about how she had seen a plot going for R120 000. My response? "Nice, that's nice" as she hastened to add that it was for 5000m^2, and it ended there. The argument came from the fact that she felt that I wasn't engaging in conversation, yet when I asked what she wanted me to say, she said she wasn't expecting anything. It was a huge blow-up, neither party was guilt-free, but the essence of the argument was mismatched expectations that were not communicated. These are very dangerous in any area of relationships, but especially where sex is concerned. This is where encouragement is important.

We often appreciate things about our spouses that we never tell them about because somehow, we think they know. "She knows I love her, why should I tell her every day?" these and other statements where people absolve themselves of saying the things that they should because they're spouses "know". Imagine if your wife always makes you food, like mine does. Then one day she decides, "he knows how to make the food, and he knows that I'd love to, so he'll figure it out" ... You may assume that the **action** of making food is different from the **action** of speaking endearment/encouragement to your spouse. The fact is both are actions, and when they are foregone because you expect that the other knows, you're setting up for disaster. So don't let your spouse guess. Tell him/her what you like and why you like it. I am yet to find someone who dislikes a positive, encouraging word of appreciation from their spouse.

- **Sexualised playfulness**- hubba-*hubba*

Playfulness is usually associated with childishness. This is why most adults are so serious, then they wonder why life is such a drag. Loosen up and get in the habit of being playful. Remember that being playful must precede sexual playfulness.

Think of the most serious person you know, imagine what it would be like if they suddenly started to unwind and be playful. For example, how would you feel if you met Vladimir Putin, and he started singing and getting into break-dancing? Wouldn't that be awkward?[33] The same awkwardness would arise from a spouse who is never playful outside the 'sack' and starts being playful during or after sex. After some time, this will become worrisome, because having two personalities is never great, and how do you justify being playful only during sex? It just seems like the playfulness is not genuine, but a means to an end.

Making play part of your life doesn't have to mean changing who you are. There are people who aren't jovial by nature. Although I must wonder what goes on in their heads? If you have the joy of the Holy Spirit and the Peace of Christ and the Blessings of The Father, why wouldn't you be jovial? Alas! We are different. So how can you become more playful?

- Consider sending text to each other while you have people around, just to remind each other how much you long to be together, alone.

- A signal that only you know the meaning too is also a nice way to introduce playful fun into your sex life.

- An appropriately inappropriate swipe at sensitive parts "during the people" as my wife likes to say. Spanking, grabbing, or a run of the hand across the chest.

- Though not my favourite, pranks really tend to make for fun times. These may not be sexual, but they have a wholistic impact on the mood between spouses.

- I've also seen that buying funny gifts, or toys is a great way to bring in some laughter. You don't even have to buy. I remember doing some grass-cutting one time and I saw a rather dull flower. I plucked it out, tiny as it were and dashed to my wife and gave it to her. Noticing that this was a playful moment, she slid it into her hair and started dancing. I joined in and the whole thing was such fun. Going back to the grass cutting, I felt revived, and I believe she was too (she was doing something around the house). As for what took place later that day, I'll leave that to imagination...

- We don't have a TV at my house, by choice. We have a set-up conducive for a TV in our lounge, but where a TV would be, I hung a piece of art my wife bought while on a work trip. What we do have are games. We believe that these are great pastimes that facilitate play. The fun we have while playing these has led to some of the sweetest memories. In fact, if you struggle with playfulness, try getting some board games that you both have an interest in. A snakes-and-ladders game once turned into a hilarious time once, with me struggling to roll a 6 to enter the game. This went on for so long that it ended up being such fun when my turn to roll came around. I ended up winning the game, with my wife being swallowed by snakes while I went up several ladders on my way to the finish line. I also recommend card games, and these can include your other family members. The effect is the same. Don't be negative and ask what games have to do with sex, try it. You'll thank me later.

- Just recently I did this to my wife. I usually wake up earlier than everyone in our house. At least 2 hours earlier. Walking past her sleeping on my way to the bathroom I noticed that she was sleeping with a rather funny face. I grabbed her phone, let in some light and took a snapshot of her. Later in the day, as she scrolled through her gallery, she noticed the picture and it became a moment of joy. You may not be taking snapshots of each other in your sleep, it may be a funny video you came across or something you saw and took a picture of. These are ways you can use to create conversation and to keep things light-hearted. Trust me when I say it spills over into your sex life. No one can enjoy sex when they're tensed up emotionally.

- This may not be a tip in and of itself, but a rather transcendent one. **Play along**. Some people (not you) get grouchy when their spouses initiate play with them. Not only does this make things sour, but it also makes their spouses less likely to initiate play in future, and to positively respond to play when they initiate it- why should they, you don't like it. I'd also recommend playing nice. Things like games can become competitive, just remember to do everything in love; lose and win lovingly.

- **Wordplay foreplay**

Can words really warm me up- texting, calling, describing...? The simple answer is YES! THEY CAN! Words are the medium by which we convey what we feel and think so that it received, interpreted and understood by others. Proper use of words can yield positive results for your marriage and your sex life interchangeably.

As described above, some of the tips for introducing a playfulness to your sex life involve the use of word. Like the tip to spice things up in the sack by use of personalised language. Get in the habit of creating and using a unique vocabulary around your sex life, this doesn't have to come out of a focused brainstorming session, but as you go through life together, the experiences you go through can be flashed back to using these words. It can be whatever word that you're both agreeable to. Sometimes this will happen naturally as you refer to a mishap that becomes a running joke for both of you.

The point is to avoid overthinking it, take the leap and use these; an inside joke between married people is always an enhancement to their relationship.

Misuse of words

Misuse of words can be more dangerous than we care to realise. One of the most destructive uses of the tongue and words are criticism and nagging. In marriage, criticism and nagging push us away from each other more than they pull us together. It's no wonder the Apostle James described the tongue in this way - "So also the tongue is a small member, yet it boasts of great things. How great a forest is set ablaze by such a small fire!" (James 3:5 ESV).

Criticism destroys the curiosity we have. As humans, we're all born with a high sense of curiosity. We want to learn new things, explore various adventures and see the world from a new perspective. What kills this is being criticised for having this curiosity and when we are discouraged by those who criticise us and attack our identity. The kingdom of God is for child-like people partly because children don't approach life through the lens of a history with disappointment. What is meant with criticism is not feedback but attacking someone's character and dressing it as feedback. For example, if I say my wife is "a terrible wife because she's **always making me late**", that would be criticism. My wife is usually culpable in the area of timekeeping, but this shouldn't be something that defines her as a wife. What is also apparent in criticism is that it usually overplays the issue. If you note the use of the word always in my example above, you will realise that it implies that my wife is never on time. This is not true, she may be late frequently, but to say she's never on time is false. Now picture such criticism being levelled at a spouse in a sexual context; you are always _____. The disappointment that comes from receiving these words is likely to kill any hopes of you having a forward-thinking discussion about your sex life.

Nagging on the other hand, is selfish. When you're repetitively asking or saying the same thing without regard for why the response is unchanged, you're insane. It's not persistence, it's pestering. Nagging is a misuse of words because a nagging person repeatedly says something to the same person despite unchanging results. A proper use of words implies true communication- where what is spoken is interpreted by the hearer to mean exactly the same thing as perceived by the speaker. What this looks like in a situation where you're not getting what you desire in your sex life is a conversation that focuses on the problem, and not the person. Realise that whatever issue you think you have as a couple, it's both of you **against** the issue. Not you against your spouse. If more sex is what you want, consider a sit-down where you explain why you feel that the frequency of your sexual encounters is an issue. Further explain what you mean when you say, 'you want more sex'. What I often find is that people are quick to complain without understanding their own feelings. When we rush to complain before a proper understanding; we are allowing our emotions to drive us, and emotions are to be handled very carefully because they are fleeting. To illustrate this, let's have a deeper look at a person complaining that they want more sex. Such a person is likely to communicate this to their spouse in the form of nagging or criticism. If they were to be asked why they wanted more sex? What does 'more sex' mean? They are rarely in a position to answer these questions truthfully. Their issue is not that they do not know what they want, but they are unaware of the reasons they want it, and the specifics on how they want it. It's no wonder why their spouses never give it to them #wink.

Rather than criticising, try reasoning with your spouse. Humans are created to pursue what they see to be valuable. A mismatch of values often yields a mismatch of pursued outcomes. The typical example is the emotionally disconnected man who always complains and nags his wife because he feels they should be having sex more often. What he doesn't realise is that his wife's needs are primarily emotional than they are sexual. If he prioritised fulfilling her emotional needs, she would be better positioned to fulfil his sexual needs. This is not a *quid pro quo* situation, but an understanding of how our roles of service feed into each other. So rather than nagging, our proverbial friend needs to understand his wife's needs and serve her in the way that best resonates with her. Then he will begin to see drastic changes in her level of desire. You see, this is the great mystery of life; you get what you want from the people you want it from by giving them what they want. So quit nagging and complaining. Adopt an attitude of gratitude for what you are getting and develop more mature means of communicating to your spouse. As a kick-start, check out the books and resources suggested in the *Parting Words Chapter*. Before then though, have a look at how you can keep *the spark* of your marriage alive in the next chapter.

Use your tongue wisely #*wink*.

In writing this chapter I could have used the words cunnilingus or fellatio. I deliberately chose not to. This is because we get caught up in the secrecy or the newness of the word that we often miss the main point. What makes oral sex uncomfortable for many is the feeling that it violates the laws of God or the spouse with whom you are doing it with. Word of advice, if anything makes you uncomfortable during or after sex, be it physical or non-physical, stop. Don't just stop at that, investigate and search yourself on why this is the case. What you'll often find is that you either have some reservations on sex as a part of marriage or something to deal with internally. Otherwise, it is perfectly normal for you to dislike certain sex acts just for the sake of not liking them.

Sex is unique to the couple who partakes in it. What makes both you and your spouse unique is what makes your relationship and sex life unique. Embracing this rather than battling each other for domination and getting the other to your side will breathe a fresh wind into your marriage. Understanding each other's differences and learning to love each other in spite of these is what sweetens your relationship. After all, love covers all sins, right? In the same way, it covers our differences and blends us into one. Just be careful that you never weaponise your tongue to destroy the other because of such differences of preference. A wise lady once said to me "What you began by speaking, must be sustained with speaking... "This is the truth of your marriage.

For me, it's amazing that my marriage began with words. I sometimes sit and consider everything in my life; my wife, our home, our son and the family we are blessed with. All of it came about because I dared to ask my wife for her hand in marriage. Simply put, everything we have, and we are in our marriage was borne out of those words. Words have great power, and we ought to use them wisely. In sex, they can greatly enhance our experience and help us create lasting memories of pleasure. Or they can be instruments of destruction and pain, the choice lies with the user of the tongue.

My advice is that you sustain what began you with words by continuing to speak. Continue to verbally express your love for your spouse, even outside the bedroom. Continue to give compliments, continue to encourage and reassure them with your words. If you have fallen in doing so, try it today. Find something you appreciate about your spouse and let them know how you feel about it. It could even be telling them how grateful you are to be married to them. Making this a habit can enhance your sex life, because truly, some people only say nice things to their spouses when they want sex- that must come to an end. Cultivate a culture of speaking loving and kind words all day, every day. This may be the start of some steamy sex (thank me later).

Chapter 8: Keeping the Spark Alive

The Spark

The concept of a spark is popularised by our likening of love and attraction to a fire. Most of us aren't consciously aware of this, but we all somehow gravitate to perceiving our love for our spouses as a fire. A personal example would be how I felt like I was "burning with love" for my wife when we started out. The fire is still there, but my ability to live in it has become better. I suppose fires best identifies with love because fire, just like love starts out small and grows into this all-consuming phenomenon that permeates all of your life. Similar to a fire, love is susceptible to being quenched by various elements[34]. So that the fire that began as a spark needs to be fed sufficient materials or resources to feed it to grow. It also needs to be protected against elements that could quench it.

The focus in this section will largely be directed toward the elements that quench the fire of love in our relationship and our sex life. This is not coincidental, but I borrowed the idea from scripture. If we look into the **Ten Commandments**, we will note that most of them are phrased in the *'thou shalt not'* form. In fact, only 1 of the 10 does not conform to this pattern, and it is the first one with a promise; "Honour thy father and thy mother: that thy days may be long upon the land which the LORD thy God giveth thee (Exodus 20:12 KJV)." Why is this the case, you may wonder? Simple, it is our nature to respond better to prohibitions than to instructions. If the commandments were phrased as instructions, i.e. I shall be thy only God instead of "Thou shalt have no other gods before me (Exodus 20:3 KJV)" it would not have the same effect. I suppose this is a consequence of Adam's fall in the Garden of Eden, because the consumption of *the fruit* meant they became aware of right and wrong, so man began to have a need to understand things in contrast, he had to be made aware of what not to do in order to appreciate what to do. So, the following portion of the chapter is largely on the quenchers of the fire, and why they are likely to quench your fire. My hope is that they show you what not to do and inadvertently teach you what to do to keep the spark that became a fire alive. On to the first quencher; familiarity.

Familiarity

In my line of work, objectivity and independence are central to one's judgement. One of the biggest threats to these is familiarity. Unfortunately, humans are wired to seek routine, and no effort is required to form bad habits/routines. It's just the way things are, or is it?

One of the biggest turn-offs in sex is a lack of creativity, but this cannot happen without some level of routine. You see this in couples who have been married for many years, they settle into a routine that sees life become monotone and boring. I am not advocating against having routines and building habits, what I want to highlight is our need to pay attention to these habits, keeping them in check and making sure that they continue to serve us. An example is the habit of regular, consistent exercise, i.e., going to the gym 4 times a week is great for one's health. However, if my goal is to build muscle and strength, going to the gym and doing cardio during my 4 sessions will not serve me well as I will build cardiovascular resistance rather than muscular strength. If muscle gain is my aim, my 4 sessions should have more of an emphasis on resistance training using weights to build strength and muscle. The idea here is that habits should always serve a greater purpose of building a life that we want, after all- habits are the building blocks of who we become.

So, one of the killers of 'the spark' in a couple's sex life is the familiarity of unchecked routines. I've been a victim of this myself. In the 4th year of my marriage, I realised a trend that saw me and my wife having sex less frequently than I would have desired. Upon conversing with her, I discovered that she too wanted to improve on this... but what was the problem?

Understanding the problem as clearly as possible was the best start to solving an issue. Too often, we want to fix issues we don't fully understand... then we wonder why things never seem to improve in our lives. So, the first thing was to understand the problem as thoroughly and honestly as possible.

    i. **The first issue was our attitudes.**

I realised that I lost confidence in making sexual advances at each instance of being turned down. My wife was also failing to get her advances reciprocated because I built a wall to protect myself from disappointment by almost turning down her advances in fear of them not materialising. This created an environment where we both thirsted for each other but struggled to communicate this. The thing about getting turned down when you initiate sex is that it decreases the likelihood of you trying next time. It also makes you apprehensive when you receive advances because some part of you is sceptical about whether such advances will result in a sexual act, while another part may just be pure spite (but men are usually not spiteful in this area, hallelujah!!!). So as a rule, say YES to each other more often. More on this in a bit.

i. Our attitudes were the results of poorly defined goals[35]

This is another one of those communication breakdown issues. Similar to having unspoken or mismatched expectations, a couple without clearly defined goals pertaining to their sex life is likely to pull in different directions as far as sex is concerned. In the case of me and my wife, we both wanted to have regular sex. As for what regular meant, I thought of regular as being the same as every day, her actions seemed to indicate otherwise. It wasn't until we had a proper sit-down conversation that we aligned our goals and expectations from our sex life... as they say, the rest is history. In fact, we are more likely to give each other reminders to reprioritise sex when life gets super busy... trust me, it can get that bad.

i. Timing was an issue.

When is the best time to have sex? Some say morning sex is the best, while the popular and secular culture has taught us that the night is the best time. So, the answer to my question depends on a couple's individual preferences. In our case, I am a morning person, my wife isn't. So, morning sex sessions are few and far between. My wife is a heavy sleeper[36] and I am a light sleeper. So, nighttime must be well timed otherwise our energy levels might give us issues.

i. Communicating our advances was mismatched.

A lot of the ideas we have about sex are influenced by Hollywood. Hollywood is not a great example of love and sex... most times, sex is portrayed as spontaneous, steamy and wild. Although this is possible, but it is not how it happens in real life. Sex is blissful, but messy. It is otherworldly, but it is a very conscious experience. It can be wild, yet peaceful also. It's amazing!!! All of this can only be possible if your advances are understood by your spouse. In our case, my wife will be touchy to try and start 'trouble'... I on the other hand am quite bland- I just come right out and say it; I want sex. So, finding some common-ground or even seeing advances from the perspective of the other was helpful here.

Sadly, our failures aggregated to create a bigger problem. Failing to iron out the above created a viscous loop. We failed to communicate and align our goals and expectations, therefore we felt dissatisfied with the state of our sex life. But we continued to suffer in silence and failed to address the issues, which made us even more dissatisfied with ourselves, and the loop continued until the sit-down conversation. But this did not happen before we bumped into more errors, like the one below- Criticism and Nagging. But the big issue here is not the failures themselves, it is how familiar we became with the status quo, almost accepting that a change was out of reach, that we did nothing. So, to round this segment up with a commandment; ***don't succumb to familiarity with failing or a bad state of affairs in your sex life; confront them and end the loop.***

Criticism and Nagging

First, let me clarify that criticism doesn't have to be directed at your spouse for it to be destructive in your marriage and sex life. You can be the subject of your own criticism, and there is nothing cool about self-depreciating talk. Another victim of our criticism is usually our sex life. Similar to the vicious loop I described above, when we are dissatisfied, we tend to speak ill of the state of affairs, and this does not restore any confidence or hope in the situation changing. Neither for us nor our spouse. The last victim of our criticism is our spouse, after all, they are the ones with us in this marriage.

Criticism and nagging are repulsive. They destroy our innate sense of curiosity and depreciate the level of confidence we have in ourselves and our relationship. I remember speaking to my wife about something totally unrelated to sex on the way to church one Sunday, and I said "Criticism does not create confidence" ... It was one of those moments when you say something that sounds profound, and you wonder where it came from because it is not something you thought much about, nor does it sound like something you'd typically say. This is when I realised that I was experiencing a '*God-moment*', where the Lord just drops something in your spirit that sets your inner man ablaze. Following these words, I realised that criticism really doesn't build-up or create any confidence. In fact, it kills confidence. The word confidence is said to be from the same root as confide, which implies the sharing of something intimate or secret. So, when confidence is being killed, how are you expecting to receive from your spouse intimacy with any regularity?

Have you ever been around or interacted with a child? They are curious, they ask tons of questions and are always eager for adventure. The world is a big playground to them. The kingdom of God is for child-like people partly because children don't approach life through the lens of a history with disappointment. When we criticise our spouse, we subliminally communicating that they are lesser-than, inadequate, and all things negative. If you've ever been criticised for something, you will usually experience disappointment, hurt, and a host of negative emotions. This is because criticism usually attacks *you* as a person and not what you have done. Similar to how God hates sin and loves the sinner, we ought to correct the wrong-doing and not bring down the wrong-doer.

You must understand that there is a difference between criticism and feedback (at least in the context of this book). Criticism attacks the person, and feedback evaluates the action. With criticism, your identity is under attack. With feedback, your actions are under review. So that my wife's burnt food doesn't make her a terrible person who wants to poison me with food, but rather a mistake made by someone who was attempting to communicate her love by making me a meal. Cheesy, perhaps, but effective. And remember to avoid giving feedback in the moment (see Chapter 9).

Another thing about feedback (we're using the correct term now) is that it is often biased, especially where sex is concerned. The pain point here is typically the lack of sex or lack of sex in a particular way. This often comes across with snide comment like "if you made an effort, we'd have sex more often" or "if you were useful around the house and with the kids, maybe I'd *give it to you* more often." This is ultimately the result of a mismatch between our expectations and reality.

Instead of criticism, make a habit of complementing your spouse. Appreciate them for what they are good at and what will tend to happen is that they will gravitate towards pursuing improvement in the area they are not good in. We all need to improve somehow, but this is harder when we're constantly reminded of it in specific areas. I don't mean you should flatter your spouse with words, or even falsely praise them- that's not what I am encouraging. What I am encouraging you to do is to take note of the things your spouse does well, even if they are unrelated to sex. Often, when our spouse does something well, we get comfortable in knowing that they do it well, and we tend to take it lightly. In my case, my wife always ensures that I eat home-cooked meals, and that I always stay well-fed. Because she's so good at doing this, I sometimes forget to tell her how much that means to me and that I treasure her efforts. Some may say that telling her these words once is enough, and she should always know that "in my heart, I appreciate what she does for me"... the truth is that humans forget very easily, and we need constant reminding of things we already know... so I try to make a habit to stop, and tell my wife that her gestures of love matter to me.

This idea of complements and building each other up with our speech is not an original idea, it's a bible-based idea. The Word says, *"Let the word of Christ dwell in you richly in all wisdom; **teaching and admonishing** one another **in psalms and hymns and spiritual songs**, singing with grace in your hearts to the Lord (Colossians 3:16 KJV)."*

The word admonishing means to reprove gently, and we reprove by dealing with the wrong-doing while treating the wrong-doer with love. We are also commanded by Scripture to do this in Psalms and Hymns, I don't know what you make of this, but I am much more likely to listen to a song (psalm and hymns) than I am to a nagging, critical spouse. The other key part of this scripture is that it says "Teaching.... one another", now the teacher is not out to destroy the person their teaching. But teaching implies an intention to add value, this is a far cry from the objective of most of our critical speech. So, a gentle reproof wrapped in well-thought-out, melodic speech is something I am willing to hear and respond well to, we all are. So, try it, putting the word of God and my humble advice to the test.

Expectations

This one is a universal quencher of fires. Somehow, we all have unspoken expectations of everyone. To prove this to you, let us consider stereotypes. Stereotypes are nothing more than expectations; we expect someone to behave a certain way because of their gender, race, age or even social status. In fact, as humans, we need these expectations in order to make sense of the world. Without them, understanding people and the world around us becomes more difficult, because our brain constantly has to form new connections when we encounter each experience. Expectations are not all bad, remember, our brains are wired to seek out patterns and routines, and so our expectations are nothing more than that.

The problem with this kind of behaviour is that it a set-up for disappointment, or fascination. How, you may ask? Easy, people are individual and unique, and not everyone will conform to our expectation of them in a given situation. For example, I am a bilingual black South African[37]. I speak English, and IsiZulu, I will not say I speak IsiXhosa (my wife's language), but I can hear it. Anyways, I speak IsiZulu, which is stereotypically a language spoken by black South Africans. So, seeing a white South African speak IsiZulu is one of the most fascinating experiences, especially in the context of our country's history with race. This is only because our expectation (stereotypically) is that a white person cannot understand nor speak our language. Seeing someone defy this is fascinating. Another not so fascinating example is that of having our friend's gossip about us, or divulge private, sensitive information that we shared with them in confidence. Our expectation is that our friends are our protectors and that they are loyal to us and are faithful to the confidentiality of our deepest secrets. When they don't live up to this, we get hurt and disappointed even to the point of losing faith in people and friendships.

The lesson from these contrasting examples of expectations not being met is that they each create a reference point for future experiences. On the side of fascination, they introduce a positive expectation, in this case; I am less likely to be surprised by seeing a white person speak my African native language, in fact, I am likely to chuckle about it while I reminisce about my initial experience that fascinated me. On the other hand, the disappointing experience with my friend is likely to make me apprehensive to friendships and the sharing of personal information, I will be closed off and always have my guard up. Another lesson about disappointment and heartbreak is that the people closest to your heart are the ones likely to break it- it is a fact. Think of it this way; if your spouse says a hurtful word about you, it is likely to hurt more than hearing the same from a complete stranger with whom you have no prior relationship. The first is called verbal abuse, the latter would be called defamation, but the substance of it is the same.

Why do I labour this point of expectations and how does it relate to your sex life? First, I do so because we need to understand that in this life ye shall have tribulation... I am joking, we need to understand that people may not always live up to our expectations. This is not their fault, but usually ours. We harbour expectations that were not communicated, sometimes we are not even aware of this. Thanks to our constant growth and evolution (not Darwinism), our preferences change, and our spouses need constant updates on these for them to keep up. In the absence of such updates, being communication, there will be a mismatch between expectations and outcomes. The mature thing is to deal with these mismatches with maturity and grace, just as God is always there to extend grace to us. No wonder the scriptures say "Love is patient" ... because you cannot handle these mismatches without patience.

I've learnt from the conversations with the people in my circle to attribute disappointment and dissatisfaction to unmet expectations. I've been disappointed many times in my life, and usually it is because what I expected did not happen. In times when I was disappointed by someone with whom I had a relationship with (not romantic), I later learnt that the disappointment and the ensuing discouragement toward pursuing the relationship further, was a result of unmet expectations. Sex is no different because sexual dissatisfaction is a result of unmet expectations. Sadly, these expectations are usually something that was never discussed prior to sexual engagement, to make matters worse.

I had an expectation that sex would be on the table every day when I got married[38]. The reality of how presumptuous my expectations had hit me in the face like a brick wall. From general tiredness to periods and period pains, there are so many valid reasons why you would go a day or two or many without. The operative word is **valid**. So, I settled for having it during the times when there was no valid reason. The issue here is the variability of 'valid' between situations, and the subjectivity of the concept. My wife's view of validity differed to mine in some cases, like the fact that I have endless energy and would still *get it on* after a long trip. Sometimes, she couldn't do that. Or I would have a super long day at work, spend hours on the road and come home to a wife who's waited all day to *'see me'*. What I learnt is this; in the absence of communicating expectations and being upfront with feeling like today *isn't the day*; dissatisfaction sets in. The other side of this lesson is to extend grace when you receive the feedback that your spouse feels like today *isn't the day*, sometimes even drawing from experience and noticing the ques. What this will do is it will enhance the quality of your relationship and reinforce your spouse's confidence in the fact that you are interested in more than just their body. It also prevents a situation where you start feeling dissatisfied with your marriage and sex life.

Dissatisfaction is dangerous, because rather than pointing you in the direction of the problem it tends to point you toward a selfish solution involving only you. It may be that you start slipping into flirty chats with women at work, or even social media connections that are less than godly in an attempt to satisfy your urges. In other instances, like my own, dissatisfaction can breed more dissatisfaction. I was in a situation where I didn't reconcile my expectations to practical reality, and it nearly destroyed my relationship. I was so focused on getting to a 7/7 that I forgot to appreciate the 4, 5 or 6/7. I know, I'm a bit of an all-or-nothing guy sometimes, but I've since learnt that this is not how relationships work, especially marriage. How did this change? I simply got to understand that concept of extending the blessing of grace to others as it has been extended to me by God. God never blesses us for us, we are always blessed to be a blessing to others. Whatever the blessing is, it is given to us for us to use it to bless others. We are loved so we can love others. Blessed financially to be a blessing to others financially. Given grace to minister grace to others. We are forgiven so we too can forgive others, in fact the scriptures teach us that we are forgiven by the measure that we forgive... this is mind-blowing.

Finally, as far as expectations go, I have learnt that it is better to ask questions than to make accusations. When our expectations aren't met by our spouses in our relationship or even sexually, we tend to get critical (as described above) to a level of accusing our spouses for the status quo. Humans are very big on self-preservation, even preserving ourselves from taking a cut of the blame for stuff that happens in our marriages. It's always someone else. But it is when we ask questions rather than levelling accusations that we build each other up along with our relationship. My mom gave me a simple parable about expectations that has paid dividends in my marriage, allow me to share it. She *said never assume the worst about your spouse. Imagine a situation where you go to work and come home way past your normal time of arrival, at the door, your wife meets you with accusing questions like' where have you been?', why didn't you call?, I've been worried sick about you, etc...' Sure it is okay for your wife to be concerned when you don't show up around the times she* **expects** *you to, but how she* **reacts** *to this is even more important. Say you arrive past your normal time because you had a flat tire on the freeway and realised that you had no cell service, or your battery died and you have no way of charging it. Added to this, the busy freeway is a hazard to your safety, so you have to signal the fast-moving cars away to avoid causing more damage. Basically, you were in an emergency situation where you had very little control until help arrived. All this, and time is passing by. Tired, and relieved to have made it through a frustrating time, you rush home to your wife before she gets more worried, then you're met at the door with salty words- how would you feel?* This short scenario that my mom painted for me taught me to avoid thinking the worst of someone and to rather ask questions than to throw accusations, so that when something

unexpected happens in my marriage, I ask why and start a conversation not a fight.

Commandment: **Always communicate your expectations**

When life gets busy

A man who loves his wife, loves himself. This may sound familiar, and cliché, but it is scriptural. The mystery of marriage begins with the merging of two people as they become one. Sadly, when we are pursuing career development or entrepreneurship, we trade-off spending time with our families. The unfortunate reality is that we all have the same number of hours in a day. In fact, this is the justice of our God, he created equity in the resources we have, so that what we become is related to our resourcefulness, and not the presence or lack of resources. The question, therefore, is not whether we have the time, but whether we make it?

I always tell my friends that I do not want to climb to the top-most rung of the corporate ladder, make tons of money and have no one to enjoy the rewards with. People often say it is lonely at the top, but this is the consequence of a trade-off that they make in pursuit of career success; they opt for this type of advancement and pay less attention to their relationships, even their marriages. In my line of work, it pains me to realise that the people who hold the highest positions in various entities are divorcees or even single parents. This is not how things should be because we are creatures of relationship, marriage being the chief most relationship ever.

One of the ways I avoid this is by being intentional to spend time with my wife, and now my son. In truth, not making time to spend with your wife is not making time to spend with yourself- make that make sense, because to me it doesn't. Who in their right mind would go a distance without spending time with themselves? People complain that they are too busy, yet they have time for TV and social media. I recently learnt about a stat that says spending 2 hours on TV/Socials a day equates to a month over a year[39]. Check the things you spend time on, usually, our time is spent on the things we prioritise... based on your recent patterns of time spent, are you prioritising your spouse? If you were to review your daily activities, is spending time with family as important to you as you think it to be?

Commandment: **Prioritise your marriage and your sex life.**

Emotional Intimacy must Precede Sexual Intimacy

Refer to chapter 2 on Adam knowing his wife.

Intimacy is key to keeping the flames of love burning in a marriage. In my view, it is the essence of any relationship. My favourite example is that of receiving an insult from a stranger versus an insult from your spouse; which hurts the most? For many of us, an insult from a spouse cut deeper, and this is because insults usually attack areas of insecurity, and these are intimate details we may have previously shared with our spouse in confidence.

Our Christian view of intimacy differs from the world because our worldview being underpinned by the Bible. Where the world attributes physical joining of two people during sex to intimacy, we look to the quality of the relationship that enhances the coming together. So that the object of intimacy is knowing each other deeply, rather than bedding each other. An interesting idea I had about intimacy and getting to know my wife was the realisation that there is a portion of her lived experience that I was not a part of pre-marriage, even now there are parts that I am not privy to like her experiences at work. Then there is the constant evolution we all go through as people, who are growing day-by-day and having our tastes and preferences change as we grow. Creating and sustaining consistent intimacy in a relationship requires spending time with each other, the question is how this can be done and what needs to be done when spending time together.

The second part of the question above is aptly covered in chapter 2. The former, is what bogs our minds the most. Some useful tips have been given in the same reference given above. But there are things to watch out for, like the *cares of this world*, whatever these may be. For most people, spending time in entertainment and social media is what eats a lot of their time. Remember that your spouse matters more than any of these. Binge-watching a series together may seem like spending time together, but you are essentially spending time in the same location having your own independent experience. It's the same thing that had my wife and I cut down on movie dates, you spend 2 hours+ in silence not connecting in any way. When knowing your spouse is your priority, becoming truly intimate with him/her, sexual intimacy becomes a means, rather than an end.

Commandment: **Get to know your spouse, pursuing to truly know him/her. Sexual intimacy will flow easier as a consequence.**

Different mating calls

As mentioned above, our means of communicating sexual advances may be mismatched because we're speaking different languages. The thing about language is that it is a medium for connection. For this to happen, it has to be understood by the one speaking it as well as the one hearing it. Our way of communicating our need for sexual connection may differ for many reasons but learning to understand each other in this area can save us a lot of frustration.

I used the concept of mating calls as a nod to the animal kingdom. I am personally fascinated by those shows that do expositions on the life of animals. One of the most interesting things about animals is how elaborate their activities are for finding a mate. I remember seeing one show where the bird being covered did a dance to lure the female bird to mate, some species even get wingmen to come to their aid. It's so wonderful to watch. The key thing from this observation is that both male and female animals of each specie naturally understand the mating requirement, i.e., the mating call, the consent and what needs to happen thereafter. For humans, this is much more complex than I can explain in a book...

We speak different love languages[40], we interpret consent in a biased manner and what needs to happen *in the act* is far more diverse than a

S. S. THABETHE

penis penetrating a vagina. For humans, mating calls are not gender specific because both husband and wife can make the call. We need much more weapons in our arsenal to succeed at sex than a simple dance. We need to learn to discern each other's mating calls, and we need to learn how to respond to these aptly.

Commandment: **learn to speak your spouse's mating language but hear it too.**

Each No is a nail in your sex life coffin.

It goes without saying that sex should be consensual even in marriage. Provided that it is built on love and mutual understanding. Just because you're married to your spouse is not an on-demand pass to all you can have sex. With this core value in place, I see no reason why a sexual advance should ever be met with rejection. In fact, I would encourage an attitude of saying yes more often.

People, especially men, like to cite scriptures that favour their cause. Such as the charge for women to submit to their husbands, or the fact that the body is the husband's. These are true and authoritative words from God. But they all come with conditions. As much as your wife's body is yours, your body is your wife's. As much as she is charged to submit to you, you are charged to love her. When I love my wife as I am called to, it makes submitting to me very easy for her. When she submits to me, it makes my loving her very easy. Likewise, when neither of us withholds our bodies from the other, it makes approaching each other for sex much easier.

The thing about hearing 'no' as a response to an advance is that it decreases your confidence in trying again. Humans don't do well with disappointment, I suppose it is our being made in the image of a never-failing God that does this to us, but when we are met with rejection, we are less likely to try again. For husbands, it bruises our egos. So, wives, please make a commitment to keep sex flowing. For wives, it communicates a larger emotional message- you do not want me. This is a generalisation I see a lot of a husband who does not

148

CRASH COURSE ON SEX FOR CHRISTIAN COUPLES

want to have sex with his wife for no apparent reason says more than him not wanting sex.

Does this mean violating each other? Not so, but let a no be for reasons other than I don't 'feel like it' or vain spitefulness.

Commandment: **Say yes more often**.

Infidelity

- An unconventional look at infidelity.

A lot of the times, victims of infidelity point the finger outwardly. They are so focused on how they have been wronged that they disregard the possibility of their own involvement in the infidelity. This may strike you as unbecoming of a believer, but marriage is a covenant of satisfying needs. We are called to satisfy each other's needs as spouses in marriage and to do so dutifully and with love. When these needs are unmet, it causes some to seek their satisfaction elsewhere.

- Our culture has stripped out the idea of duty from the institution of marriage, making it an airy-fairy institution of chocolates and roses – it is not. Marriage is hard work that requires maturity and being enlightened by the spirit of God. Teaching on divorce, what did Jesus say to the disciples when they said, "it is better not to marry"? Scripture says "But he said to them, "Not everyone can receive this saying, but only those to whom it is given. (Matthew 19:11 ESV)". In this passage, Jesus dealt with a legalistic question of divorce by providing a heart perspective. The crux of the question sought his [heavenly] opinion on divorce and potentially, how that fared against the law set by the great Moses (people and their heroes' #sigh) ... Effectively, they wanted God's design to conform to man's preferences. Yet the original plan of God for marriage was for it to remain unbroken until death. But because of the hardness of men's hearts, the certificate of divorce was instituted. We are able to stay married, not because we are innately able to stay the journey, but because the giver [of strength] is God Himself, by His empowering Spirit. Jesus would not say this if it weren't true, because in our own strength, marriage is an impossible dream. After all, we are preaching the finished article of the Christ-church relationship.

The word also makes the first mention of a husband-and-wife relationship in the context of satisfying needs. It is important to understand this, it's called the law of first mention. Basically, when you read the Bible, in order to understand a concept, you have to look for the form in which it is presented when it was first mentioned (usually in the book of Genesis). The way in which it was used/mentioned there is almost always the original intention of God concerning it. So, in terms of marriage, we see it mentioned at the back of God saying 'it is not good'... then he made Eve to address this deficiency. What it tells us is that Eve (who typifies wives), is always brought into a man's life to help. My understanding of help is that it is given to someone who **needs** it. And boy do men need help. I remember in our initial days of dating; I had stumbled upon this concept, and I asked my wife what she needed from me. Her answer was genius, yet simple. She said she needed me to love her. Returning the question to me, my response to her was "respect". So, we have prioritised these in our marriage. But secondary to these is affection for my wife and sex for me. Dr Myles Munroe once said that the need of a man is sex. He was right, men need sex. What they need more is respect (being honoured). Now this entire mini-expository is to point this out; infidelity may be the result of unmet needs. It is not a rule, and even if it was, there would be exceptions...

You cannot control how your spouse reacts, but you can control how you react and how you act. So many women want to be empowered these days, they want to be equal to men and they convince themselves that men and women are the same. We are not. And these silly trends that claim to be empowering women are disempowering them. They also make you unattractive to men because you are becoming disrespectful in the name of equality. Don't let the world fool you, it has nothing good to offer you. Even if you're called names, just remember this: we are most empowered when we live in our God-given purpose. When men love their wives (and none other) and when wives submit to their husbands.

- It would be a disservice to your marriage to disregard the causes of infidelity and eventual divorce in other people's marriages. Most times, Christians are guilty of a perpetual overdose in positivity and faith, that they lack the practicality of dealing with life's basic issues. We see this in money matters- people will go into bad financial decisions and give the immortal "the Lord will provide" phrase. Whenever you say the d-word, married people shrink and tense up. It's as if you're pronouncing it on their marriage. But a closer look at divorce, it's indicators and eventual causes serve much for married people to learn and apply (or avoid applying) in their own marriages.
- Some of the biggest threats to marriages today include, but are not limited to the following issues:

- Financial issues

- Sexual issues

- Infidelity

The first issue requires some training in the handling of money. For that, there is a host of literature on the subject that is worth considering. I'd personally suggest some Dave Ramsey for a Christian/biblical perspective on finances with a slap of practicality. I'd also suggest 'I will teach you to be rich' by Ramit Sethi, if you have a palate for secular writers. For those proverbial thinkers out there, the age-old *The Richest man in Babylon* is a great start. The point is, I won't be dealing with this directly in this text, but I would strongly caution you against neglecting this area as it has the potential of causing much trouble in marriage.

The second issue is why I am writing this book in the first place. Sex can be a huge pain point in many people's marriages. Without the mechanisms presented here and in other read-worthy texts, many more marriages would 'hit-the-rocks'. The fact is that sex is at the heart of marriage by virtue of it being so binding on a spiritual, emotional and physical level. Very few activities, if any, can boast such a transcendent effect on life. However, the lack of sex is also a great indicator of issues elsewhere in the marriage. Since sex begins in the mind (see chapter 2), it is easy to see why anything that occupies the mind unduly can have a negative effect on a couple's sex life. Financial distress is one very common culprit.

The third issue is one that concerns me most. I have seen it in my own family, in the lives of people around me and read about it quite a number of times (I'm assuming you have too). One gentleman said the demon behind infidelity/promiscuity/sexual sin will be the most honoured among demons because it is responsible for so many falls in the lives of Christians.

STI's and STDs are real. They can wreck relationships, homes and even lives. I think infidelity is one thing that makes you realise how your marriage connects you with other people. Your family, your extended family. All these people are affected by your actions. This is one of the considerations that those who are victims of infidelity in marriage make. Yet no one should stay in a marriage at the cost of their safety and wellbeing. This is usually what the world teaches, hitting the road as soon as you find out about cheating. It is worth considering though, the impact of the decisions you make. Sometimes, the cheating could lead to a conversation with ourselves on what it is that we contributed to the cheating. It's hard to imagine yourself being responsible for the actions of your spouse in the context of infidelity.

The kingdom of God has a different set of principles compared to the world. Most times when the question of infidelity comes up for discussion, the world is keen to resort to the annulment of the marriage. The d-word is so common that even believers have come to a season where it is an option regardless of the situation. What I mean by this is that divorce has become so common that we rarely take the time to consider the biblical perspective on it, even when we give advice to others. Where the issue of divorce arises due to infidelity, most people are quick to refer to the response of the Lord Jesus to the question of whether divorce is 'okay' (See Matthew 19:3 – 12). Most people get caught up on the proviso that permits divorce, being sexual immorality. But not as many consider that the Jesus said "what God has joined together, let no man separate" ... The scriptures also say that the institution of divorce only came about because of the "hardness" of men's hearts. In other words, divorce is a construct of a hard or unforgiving heart, which separates what God has put together. I am not advocating for people to stay married with unfaithful spouses, I am making a case for slowing down before opting for divorce. If the guilty spouse shows remorse, consider counselling and mending the relationship. Having experienced divorce from the perspective of a child, it is quite brutal. From what I heard from my parents; it seems even more brutal. Usually, those who are honest post-divorce, will admit that divorce does not make any of the influencing factors of their divorce go away. This is why people who divorce, are likely to repeat this if they marry again.

Insulating your marriage against infidelity and unfaithfulness is a wide topic, but it requires simple and applicable principles for success. There is a saying among IsiZulu-speaking people that says "Umona usuka esweni", directly translated to say, "envy begins in the eye". Our eyes are the windows through which we perceive the world. Sadly, they are the Achilles tendon of many a man. One look at a beautiful woman, and the man loses his faithfulness. In my observation, infidelity usually finds its roots in untrained eyes. So, I will share with you what was taught to me as a young man: look up or look down.

This can be viewed figuratively or literally. In a literal sense, your eyes should not wander to places they need not be. If your struggle in this area, get in the habit of looking up or looking down or anywhere else other than gazing at the temptation. In a figurative sense, make a covenant with your eyes to not look at a woman lustfully. This is not my wisdom, it is scripture. "I promised myself never to <u>stare with desire</u> at a young woman. (Job 31:1 CEV)" We see clearly that it does not say don't look at women, like some would lead us to believe. That is *churchianity*[41], not godliness. My personal rule is to look to see and not to gaze. One of my friends used to say you can undress a woman to nakedness with your eyes; he was right. Some men struggle so much with this that a look at a woman's chest can send them into a frenzy of unclean thoughts. If this is you, I advise you to seek a trusted partner with whom you will get into prayer and fasting to break this spirit, because it is an unclean spirit.

Commandment: **Commit to being faithful to your spouse and the purity of your marriage**.

The best apology

It is impossible to go through life with your spouse without hurting them. For those at the initial stages of married life, hurting your spouse may seem an impossible task. So let me simplify the concept for you in a phrase... the people who occupy your heart are the ones with the capability of hurting it. A negative word spoken by a stranger has no effect on you, but if the same were to be done by your beloved wife or husband- it would cut very deep.

The thing about communication, then, is that it allows you to identify the areas where you've caused pain to your beloved. Affording you the opportunity to course correct. However, I always say that the best apology is changed behaviour. If you are to apologise for the same mistake repeatedly, your apology loses meaning each time. The best approach is to apologise, then be intentional about avoiding the very thing that caused your loved one hurt in the first place. If you are to keep the flames of love and sexual attraction burning in your marriage, be forever at work in changing the behaviours that quench this fire.

A message of hope for those who've had their spark put out- *7-day sex challenge*

Keeping the spark alive requires consistent action from both husband and wife. Having a clearly defined objective is key. Simply stating that you want a better sex life is not enough. What do you want to be better, why do you want it so? Or how can that be achieved? Better is not definitive enough. Another element is the consistency with which you apply good principles; this is couple-dependent. 3 times a week might do it for one couple, and not for the next. Action speaks louder than words because it creates a precedent. If I say I want my wife and I to have sex daily, I need to back it up with action. If I don't, she's likely to not trust me when I say I have an intention to improve our marriage or even our sex life.

Perhaps you've read this chapter and realised that you and your spouse have fallen victim to one of the quenchers detailed above. All hope is not lost, your relationship and your sex life can be revived again. I challenge you to look into your heart and confront what has been holding you back. Even if it seems that your spouse has held you back from trying to piece back the wreckage, realise that it may be your own fears that keep you from this pursuit. Maybe your marriage has been struck by infidelity, you may be the victim or even the perpetrator; realise that there is no sin that cannot be forgiven by God through Jesus Christ, and He has empowered us by His Spirit to minister the same grace and forgive those who 'trespass against us'... it sounds much easier than it is, but it is the truth of God's word. If there be a willingness to continue the journey, make the move, have the sit-down conversation and rekindle the spark. If the situation permits, I encourage you to go on the 7-day sex challenge. Throughout this 7-day period, I want you to initiate sex with your spouse at least once a day. It doesn't have to be anything complicated, but it has to be consensual. Speaking about it beforehand will help, as your spouse will know what to expect and what it is you're trying to achieve. It will also hold you accountable to fulfilling this commitment, but also rebuild your spouse's confidence in your willingness and ability to live up to your word. Try it and let me know what happens. But remember this, it is better to resolve conflict than to dissolve relationships. This is a statement I heard from someone preaching and I thought it to be so profound because many times we think that dissolution is the solution when conflict resolution is.

Resolve to make positive changes for the better of your marriage. Resolve to encourage each other rather than criticising each other. Taking note that you do not 'let the sun go down on your anger'... Anger is punishment you laude onto yourself for someone else's behaviour, and no one wants that. So, learn to forgive, because if you don't, you will struggle, even with sex.

In the next chapter, we will be looking at a few ideas around sex. Some of these are likely to help you in keeping the spark alive. So, keep reading.

Chapter 9: Some Ideas on Sex

This chapter is dedicated to the person who is so overwhelmed with the area of married sex, they don't know where to start. It is also useful to the one who has enjoyed this gift so long, that they're considering spicing things a bit. Change is always good for reviving a lukewarm sex life.

The aim is the encourage you to avoid making sex a chore. Make it a part of your lifestyle and an ingredient in your arsenal of intimacy. Unshackle your mind from the years of abstinence (or promiscuity for some) and truly understand that sex is a gift to be enjoyed with your spouse, however many times you want and however you want- consensually. Below are some ideas that relate to sex and how they can be used to bring in some much-needed flavour in your sex life as a married Christian.

Sexting

Just like in many areas of life, we let the world dictate the *'how'* in things that originate in the church. Sexting is another tool in the sex arsenal that God has given us for sexual arousal.

Sexting refers to sexual talk between a couple using text or instant messaging. This is a powerful way to engage the imagination and capture the attention of your lover. When you receive a message telling you that your lover is thinking of you and desires you sexually it ups the ante on the arousal. For the husband, a text like this can have him fly through work just to get home to his wife, so use the methods sparingly to avoid accidents #wink. For the women, it is also very useful, because their arousal takes more time. It needs to simmer gently for a long time.

Picture the effect if you are to get to work, or wherever you're spending your day away from your beloved. You text them to tell them you have arrived and that you are safe. You then follow this up with a message reminding them how much you love them and how much you look forward to getting back to or with them later that day. You add in a fantasy of your own liking, something you have done or want to try. You can even give them a '*5-star rating*' on their performance in the evening or morning prior, let them know how much you look forward to doing it again. All this is sexting.

With instant messaging, you can also throw in some emoji's... there are some that are universally accepted as sex symbols (i.e., the eggplant for the penis and the peach for you know what...). You can make your own, a heart emoji could mean 'I Love you' for one couple, and 'Let's get it on tonight' for another... the key is to bring in your own creativity and make this your own.

This is usually met with scepticism by many, but the sending of 'nudes' is also a tool worth considering. I've met a couple where the wife periodically shares some intimate pictures of herself to her husband while he is away at work just to "brighten up his day." Personally, I have reservations about cyber security and the risk of the picture landing in someone else's device. An instance of such a leak happened when a respectable church lady mistakenly shared a 'nude' on a church group... I think this was before the time of 'delete for everyone' on WhatsApp. This is one of the disasters that can happen with sending nude pictures of each other, and the sad thing is that the unintended recipients can't unsee it. If this doesn't scare you enough to avoid it, then try installing software that will protect you and your spouse's personal images. It is worth considering the approach of downloading a separate application that you can use solely for connecting with your spouse or even for the sending of these pictures; a pop-up notification from said app is sure to get your lover's fire going.

Sharing of sexual texts and pictures does not need to be vulgar, or even explicit. If you've 'done it' on the couch, you could literally take a picture of the couch, and send it to you beloved with no caption. This may garner interest, and solicit a call to enquire, then you can finish you story and tell them what plans you have for the couch. My point here is to get creative and remove the stigma of a dull sex life among Christians. I know that this might be an abstract idea for many, but I know of people who are convinced that we have to 'say grace' before we engage in sexual activity. There is nothing wrong with appreciating the gifts of God before enjoying them, but I can imagine the turn-off of a person praying in tongues for hours before actually doing the deed. Just to have their husband/wife dose off to sleep. Don't do things that take the juice out of sex, make it lively and enjoyable. Keep things light-hearted and you'll likely improve your relationship and your sex life.

Quickies

One of the greatest blessings that came with COVID-19[42] was the arrangement of working from home. My wife and I were locked down together as we were in the same line of work. To add to this, lockdown was within the first 6 months of us getting married, so that should explain a lot (#wink). But one of the most thrilling discoveries was the concept of quickies.

Quickies, as the name might imply, are quick sexual encounters. A lot of the precursors to penetrative sex are thrown out the window and you dive straight to the point (pun intended). No foreplay, no simmering, just sex. Usually, it doesn't last as long because you're in-between meetings, or stealing a moment while there are guests in the other room. Adding these to your repertoire is sure to keep things fiery.

One of the implementation ideas here is having some essentials always on hand. Some lubrication of your choosing, a blanket if you're so inclined and a sense of humour. I remember my wife making use of a bed cover that was in our en-suite as a foundation for a quick romp during a 'break' while working from home. We also had a guest during this one, so we had to be quick, and stealth was a no brainer. The fact that we were the only ones who knew what we had done was also key to a later steamy session. But the joy of looking at each other with beaming eyes as if to say "I know what we were up to in the other room" is priceless.

Sleep Naked

Don't go to bed adorned with layers of clothing like a cabbage. If you are prone to layering up on account of the weather, try warming up with your spouse. Jump into bed naked and cuddle up together. Without much force, this is bound to charge your sexual batteries to 'full' in seconds. This practice is a simple yet effective means of letting your spouse know that sex is on the table anytime they please. Nothing says *'you're welcome to play with me'* like a fully undressed spouse rubbing against you with their skin.

Planned Sex

Planned sex is still sex. I felt it necessary to repeat the sub-heading for this one. Popular culture has caused us to overstate the value of spontaneity. When we see those movies where there is a 'lovemaking' scene, it always seems to be in the moment and unplanned. Even if there is a conversation about sex prior to the act itself, it always seems to be smooth, passionate and the people partaking always seem to be in sync. This is not coincidental. You should remember that the actors are casted after rigorous evaluation, and one of the evaluations includes a chemistry test.[43] This is a test to determine whether the actors in question have chemistry. What bogs my mind is that the test involves professional actors who are supposed to 'act as if they have chemistry', this doesn't happen very often in married couples. Sure, you may have chemistry and have your attraction be near palpable to those around you, but sex in real life isn't that. The chemistry can be built over time, and the smoothness of the sexual act is also developed through a journey of moments of silliness, giddiness and mishaps. All this is a part of the journey and that is what makes your sex life *yours*.

As we grow, so do our responsibilities. With that comes the element of allocating our time to various priorities. For some, this includes having to plan out sex. This may seem like it sucks the life out of the experience, but humour me this: if you have a planned wedding, as most weddings are, does it take anything away from the grandeur of that moment when you publicly commit to each other and make a covenant of love? The experience of my own wedding convinces me the answer is *no*. I had the best time on my wedding day, I smiled so much that my jaws were raw by the night of my wedding. I was so exhausted, just by smiling. So how about applying the same principle to sex. Especially when you realise that you have put other things before the wellbeing of your marriage and sex life. Put in a diary, or a calendar. Paste it on your bedroom wall. Tell each other how much you anticipate this moment, this adds to the excitement.

Some key facts that may persuade you to plan out time for sex include the fact that it shows commitment to intimacy with your spouse. Our life is measured through time and planning to spend time with each other doing anything is a means of spending life together. What this also does is builds anticipation for the sexual experience. This is good news, especially for the women because they require some 'warming up' mentally before sex. Don't be surprised to come home and have your spouse jump on you because they couldn't wait for the 'moment'.[44]

Weekly/monthly/quarterly reviews

We're guilty of partitioning our lives in a way that leaves the good stuff about our world of commerce at work. In an attempt to keep business away from play, we lose out on some hacks that can greatly improve our lives. What I am referring to here is the art of doing self-reviews periodically. In my line of work, we have checklists, reviews and various quality assessments to ensure that our product is of the highest quality. What this does is that it forces us to become more efficient, and more attentive to the things that matter most in our process of producing valuable outcomes. In relationships, we coast through with the subconscious expectations that things will work out because we are in love. This could not be further from the truth. Marriage is work, and our sex lives are no different. If we are to become better in any area, including sex, we ought to set out a vision and a means of monitoring progress towards realising that vision. This may sound cold, but it is good to step back and assess where you are once in a while.

This may sound out of place, but you may be convinced by what God did in creation. Each time He had made something, the bible says, 'God saw that it was good'. This shows us that God took time to see what he had done and to evaluate it, hence He would remark that it is good. If this approach works for God, why wouldn't it work for you? Least of all in the area of sex.

A practical means of doing this is to have weekly dates with your spouse where you catch-up on where you are in life. This was recommended to me by a good friend of mine, and we have tried to keep to it with my wife. During such dates, you can discuss where you are relationally first, then sexually. This is because much of the issues that manifest in sexual dysfunction are manufactured in relational dysfunction.

SWOT analysis

This is one of those things I bring into my life from work. We learnt about the S.W.O.T analysis in 'varsity. It is a model of analysing **S**trengths, **W**eaknesses, **O**pportunities and **T**hreats in business. In the context of sex and marriage, this might look like this.

- Strengths would be the areas of your sex life that are worth commending, things where you believe to be doing well in.
- Weaknesses are usually a direct opposite of strengths. These are the areas where you are not doing well in.
- Opportunities are circumstances that present possibilities to do or achieve something. In my experience, our weaknesses present opportunities from growth, so that weaknesses in the SWOT analysis can be transferred to opportunities.
- Threats are things that threaten what is being analysed. In our case, this is our sex life and marriage by extension. Typically, weaknesses are also a great place to begin when looking for threats. As a weakness is likely to be a threat to a great sex life.

The thing about this is that it is subjective. So that a strength in one spouse's eyes can be viewed as a weakness in the others. Though the possibility of this is remote. This is why it is important to perform this analysis individually and get together with your spouse to 'compare notes'.

Some key areas of evaluation where sex is concerned include, but are not limited to the following: frequency, intensity, sex positions, level of adventure in sex, lasting longer, sexual furniture, quality of communication, external forces (i.e. distractions, children, work, in-laws, etc...), who initiates sex, Consumption of Porn, Limiting beliefs about sex, declining health, long-distance relationship, sex toys and a host of others you can consider.

I'm wrong...

This is something I learnt in the early stages of my marriage. In fact, it was borne out of the speech my friend gave at my wedding. In it, he advised that as the husband, I must always be the one initiating reconciliation and being ever ready to say, "I am sorry". The gist of this advice was for me to lead by an example of forgiveness and humility. What then became of it was my understanding that I should assume that I am wrong in every argument/ altercation or discussion where right and wrong is being considered between me and my wife. This doesn't mean I am a pushover or a yes man. But it means that I always default to seeking the reasons why my wife would believe me to be in the wrong for a given situation. Admittedly, it is not an easy thing to practice, because it calls for humility of the kind that challenges your own self-righteousness.

What it has done is that it has saved me a number of fights that could have blown out of proportion and had our home sur for hours. Assuming a position of humility and putting the other first makes one humble enough to accept correction for wrong and to receive feedback about how their actions have made the other feel. This is the opposite of what we tend to exhibit in our behaviour, seeking only to defend our righteousness in every argument. What this also does is that it insulates you from fighting to prove that your spouse is wrong. This is because an argument is rarely about convincing the person you're arguing with that you are right, but mostly about showing them that they are wrong.

Such behaviour is bad for your relationship, because arguments and fights are very good at quenching the fires of romance in any household. So, avoid unnecessary quarrelling and adopt a position of humility. It will do your marriage much good and your sex life even better. This is not to say apologise so you can get sex, but a call to the pursuit of harmony in the home.

The don'ts of an *ideal sex life*

1. **The worst thing you can do is to criticise a sexual experience moments after it has happened.** Delay has always been a great tip in this area. Most of us feel a sense of injustice when we reserve

our comments after a 'bad' experience. Being radical can cost you in the area of sex, because the whole experience is still fresh. A word of advice: take a timeout. Ponder your experience and align your words. Nothing is more damaging than a word misspoken by a spouse with good intention. Also consider the environment, you can't try to fix wrongs when you yourself are not entirely blameless. The point is that feedback should be well-timed and given in love.

1. **Pause before you speak**. The Word says, "When words are many, transgression is not lacking, but whoever restrains his lips is prudent (Proverbs 10:19 ESV)." What we can gather from this scripture is that it is wise to tame your tongue/lips. Avoid vain speaking because you expose yourself to sin (transgression). In the context of marriage and sex, rather take a timeout than hurt your spouse with unkind words spoken in the heat of the moment. This may even help you in areas other than sex. Much of the damage done in relationships is with words, so use them carefully. We discussed this in the previous chapter, so I will not labour it further.

1. **Morning after**: The morning after is a great time to reflect on your experience the night before. For those who want to do it in the morning, your 'morning afters' could be evenings or during the day. During this time, reminding each other of your experience often sparks the fire anew and keeps you both simmering. Depending on the situation (wisdom helps here), you can discuss what you liked, what worked and what didn't. Capitalise on those moments when the fires are burning hot, build on this. As a side note to the ladies, sex hurts in the early days or even when you spend a long time apart. So, take things slow, and keep the hiatus short.

1. **Don't use sex as a weapon**- This is an area where the women are usual culprits. Because of the biological reason that men tend to want sex all the time (though there are women who could rival this claim), wives often use sex as a weapon. I like to call this *carrot-and-stick sexuality*. This is when either of the two spouses (usually the

Women) use sex as a reward to get the other spouse to do the things they want, when they want. In the case of women, the poor man will bend over backwards just to 'get some'. This is a *huge* don't. Not only does this lessen the value of your sexual experience, but it is also a complete misunderstanding of sex as it should be. Sex is not about giving your spouse a good time as many women will say things like ... "If you do this, I'll show you a good time tonight" or words like "you're definitely getting it tonight..." after he does something for you. When sex becomes a reward, how do you expect that man to behave when sex is presented to him by someone else without the arm-long preconditions you set? This is not to say he'd be guiltless if he fell for the extramarital sexual advances, but rather to show you how the wife can play a part in creating a conducive environment for infidelity (see chapter 8 on infidelity). Early on in our marriage, my wife and I decided never to use sex either as a reward and/or a punishment. This practice of rewarding 'good behaviour' with sex and punishing 'bad behaviour' with depriving sex should not be found among believers.

1. **Nagging is not the answer**. Oddly enough, our brains are wired in a way that gravitates to repetition for emphasis. What this becomes is nagging when it's played out in real life. Ever had a person say something to you in an inaudible way? You typically signal that you couldn't hear them of put on a confused face. What usually follows is that the person repeats what they said in a louder tone and sometimes with a bit more tempo. Their assumption is that a louder tone will transfer their message better. This is what we do when we have been asking for some change be it in sex or other areas of our lives. We think that by constantly repeating our wants and desires for more, better or even less sex our partner will fold, and eventually listen. This is not the answer.

Rarely do we change our behaviour because we have heard something more times than we'd want to. We're just not wired that way. Repeating your message isn't the answer. Asking questions is. Most times a change in behaviour is difficult for reasons that are not apparent to the one beckoning for a change. Let me make an example... if your spouse has a habit of biting their nails, telling them to stop is not likely to make them stop. Doing so repeatedly won't change anything either.

1. **NEVER** shame your spouse or your sex life publicly. What has been my observation is that people who feel that they are not getting what they want out of their marriage, especially when it comes to sex, are brutal in their description of their spouse. This may be subtle, and probably done with the intention of coercing your spouse to change but hear it from me: it never works. Although this can be nit-picked, but I got some sound advice in the initial stages of my marriage. It happened so subtly that I have trouble remembering where I heard it from. But it goes something like this: "Your wife (or husband) is always the best wife (or husband) in the world when you're talking about her to others. You can fix your problems behind a closed door when it's just the two of you" What this advice can imply is that you should over exaggerate your spouse's goodness in the eyes of others, but the true meaning of it is that we ought to protect our spouses. Their reputation should never suffer assault at our hands. In my case, my wife is the best person in the world, even if we left home fighting. What this does is that it creates confidence between you as a couple that regardless of the storms, you will always be each other's supporters. The practicality of this is a challenge, because you have to find the good things about your spouse and amplify these while minimising their short-comings.

From an outsider's perspective, it is embarrassing to hear someone berate their spouse, especially when it comes to sex and the spouse is sitting right there. It just makes you wonder if this person will ever get any sex, because their actions are like pouring fuel to a fire. The wrong kind of fire, even.

Spicing up your Sex life

Gamifying sex may seem a far-fetched notion. But introducing play into a rather difficult area of your relationship may prove to be revolutionary. As a suggestion, write out a few of your fantasies or sexual desires (9 or so). Then put them in a box and take one out each day for 7 days. The remaining 2 can be for day 8 in the morning and evening. That way, there's anticipation, suspense, and novelty- especially when you are trying something new. The key is to have a willingness to try and a cooperative spouse. As a rule- stop immediately when anything feels uncomfortable (Chapter 9).

There's something about introducing an element of gaming in anything. Consider the use of imprinting objects on urinals in an airport, this was said to reduce cleaning costs by more than 20% as men tended to have less instances of 'splashback' when they had something to aim at with their urine stream (Evans-Pritchard, 2023). What we can deduce from this is that introducing a clear target and 'gamifying' the pursuit of it works wonders, especially for men as we are driven by the chase. Take advantage of this and gamifying things to spice up your sex life.

You can have your own version of pulling fantasies out of a box, perhaps you can do this in a situation where only the spouse choosing from the box knows what is to be done. Introduce some music that will be a lifetime reminder of your experiences together, wear a sexy piece that accentuates parts of your body that drive your spouse wild (i.e., lingerie). The aim is to keep things light-hearted. It is important to note is that fun for me and my wife is something different to you and your spouse. Find the things you both enjoy, and use these to your advantage. Remember that it should be consensual, done with love and mutual respect.

A couple that showers together, stays together

It was the week prior to our wedding when my wife had a Xhosa version of a bachelorette known as *Amabaso*. The point of this wonderful event is to gather married women from the community which my wife grew up and have them celebrate that she's going to be entering the journey of marriage. The fun part of this event is that there is a time for giving of gifts, and the sharing of wise words from the women who have walked the walk. One such piece of advice was that my wife ought to 'bath/shower with her husband'. When I heard about this, you can imagine my excitement as a yet to be married man who had the unfulfilled sexual urges. Alas! When we got married, we kept to this advice and for almost 2 years [45] of our marriage we washed together every morning and evening.

What taking a wash together has done is that it has made us aware of each other's presence. I get to see, touch and feel my wife's naked body at least twice a day. This means that there is never a day when I am too busy to admire and appreciate this beauty, whatever this appreciation ends up being #wink.

The other thing about this is that it is hard to be in the shower or bathtub with someone you're not talking to. Especially for us, because COVID-19 lockdowns took place months into our marriage. So, bath-times weren't necessitated by work related travels. We washed up when we wanted to, and this had to be agreed upon. If any one of us was angry at the other, running the bath without inviting the other would be a clear sign of trouble. Further, squeezing into a tiny tub when you're angry at your spouse and giving them the silent treatment will break that silence very quickly. My wife and I could never escape each other, the bathroom became a spot for reconciliation, and some initiation of some of the most mind-blowing make-up sex. It's amazing what the simple practice of washing up together will do for your marriage and sex life. Some times our sense of adventure was called to action because the bedroom was too far, and in the moment, we both wanted nothing to come between us #wink.

Give this practice a try, and let me know how it works out for you and your spouse.

Speaking in Code

At the time of writing this book, our son was only months old and the immediate need for code words was not an issue for us. But using code words for sex can be a fun way to keep the spark alive. The idea that only the two of you know what you refer to when you use that word makes things spicy. We have our ways of communicating about sex that no one else would notice, I even take the opportunity to give my wife a light spank in public spaces just to remind her that I am 'watching her'... but in all this, we have a lot of fun. You'll find us giggling at our inside jokes that only we understand. Sometimes, we finish each other's sentences or say one word and the other understands exactly what is meant. This is something to aspire to, and to pursue.

Find your own means of communicating your desire for each other, create your own language so you can keep the sexual fires burning, even in the presence of others. It will bring you together and keep you both simmering with passion for each other.

Our 30-day Sex Challenge

During the writing of this book, I tried a challenge of writing everyday throughout the month of March 2023. I'd been writing this book for months and I was battling inconsistency, Self-doubt and general procrastination. Basically, I was Overthinking the writing process. I stumbled upon this 'write everyday' challenge listening to a Tim Ferris show on Spotify where I learnt that being a writer isn't about being great at it every day or even writing beautifully each day. A writer is someone who writes consistently. So that was my aim; to write consistently. It didn't matter if it was a paragraph, a sentence, a chapter (though it never got that deep), or even a word. As long as I kept the writing in motion. 31st March came by, and I had kept to the challenge. My wife and I took time to celebrate my success, during which the conversation of my consistency brought into question our consistency in sex. In that time, we were blowing hot-and-cold as far as sex is concerned. The desire was there, but it wasn't backed by action. We'd been a few months into parenthood, work got in the way and life got busier by the day. During our celebration, my wife cheekily said *"how about you bring that streak on me"*... Along with other words that are not fit for public consumption #wink. On the 1st of April 2023, there was no time for April fool's jokes- we got down to business. On the next day and every day thereafter. Inadvertently, this became a sexual revival, and our relationship was taken to another level of closeness. I learnt so much from that I decided to include some of my takeaways from that challenge in this book....

1. Sex can bring to light areas of your relationship that aren't doing well

In our journey to through the challenge, a lot of areas and pain-points I our relationship were revealed. I won't sell-out on my wife on this, but I realised that sex truly requires a healthy relationship. So much so that to succeed in the challenge will require some 'housekeeping' as far as your relationship is concerned. We found ourselves dealing with things that had been causing us heartache in silence, like the issue of our sex life and where we wanted it to be. We also spoke about life, our aspirations and how we can support each other in pursuit of these. Surprising what sex can do for your relationship, you truly become one.

1. Sex brings you face to face with who you are (selfish out the window)

This is probably a confession piece of my own. During the streak, I knew that sex was a guarantee on a daily, so my mind got an opportunity to delve into other areas. One such area was how my pursuit of sex, and more sex was about me. I was being selfish in that I cared more about what I wanted than what my wife wanted. This may seem odd, but the epiphany hit me in those moments when I was exhausted but still had to minister to my wife's sexual needs regardless of how I was feeling. In those moments, I wondered whether she has to do the same for me after a long day *slaving away* with house chores while I sat back and had my feet up in relaxation. I wondered how she felt when persisted to pursue sex as more of a priority than her emotional needs. I wondered and wondered but it all came down to this: I needed to afford my wife more grace in the area of sex, especially as it pertains to physical exhaustion. I also learnt to appreciate her self-denial when she insisted on us doing the deed despite her having good reason not to. This was when I came face-to-face with my selfishness.

1. Sex brings you closer (physically, emotionally and spiritually)

The physical closeness in sex goes without saying. But the streak brought to light so much conversation that led to emotional and spiritual revival in our marriage. We got to chat without the weight of doubting whether we would engage sexually, we got to deal with issues that plagued us, as stated above. We even realised the need to revive some old practices of ours concerning our prayer life as a couple and as individuals. I don't claim that having sex will do this for everyone, but this was my experience. Part of the challenge was a review of myself as I went through, and even after. What I can say is that it shed so much light into our marriage such that my wife is in a different stratosphere emotionally and relationally. I believe and feel that we are more like what it is to be **one**. It is so difficult to put this into words, you have to experience it for yourself.

1. Our reasons for not doing better in our sex life are usually baseless excuses.

In doing the *30-day challenge, I learnt that* it made me power through the excuses. I learnt that one is less likely to play defence with *'the goods'* because their mate said or did something to them. I think it forces you to learn how to forgive quickly. I realise that having periods of coldness and not talking to each other because we are having a fight would not have served us well during the streak. How would it have been possible to have sex with someone you're still giving the silent treatment?

The streak came at a time when I was getting back to exercise, work was approaching a peak and I was back to regular travel to work- on a 125cc motorbike that struggled to go past 90km/h without clocking the rev' meter. I was tired, but I pushed on because I believed that there was good to the streak. In a sense, it was a means of expressing love unselfishly. From what I could tell, my wife was having the time of her life. Not without her own hurdles, she was fresh out of a 4-month maternity leave, and was juggling getting back to the grind of a *9-to-5* in addition to her new duties as a breast-feeding mom. She was trying to get a handle on exercise, dietary changes, and being a mom. Tired was a buzzword, but the streak had to continue. None of us had time for listening to excuses, so none of us ever complained. This was evidence that reasons such as "I am tired, I don't feel like it" or other similar reasons are just baseless excuses. If you were to dig deeper, you'd find that you are just being selfish, somehow. In my case, I learnt that my saying "no" to my wife's advances means I am imprisoning her to burning passion that only I can release her from, yet I expect faithfulness. This is not to give her a pass of being unfaithful, but to illustrate how serious it is to deprive each other our bodies- anyways, the word say they don't belong to us. How would you feel if something of great help that belonged to you was kept from you in your time of needing it? This is the same thing we do when we deprive our spouses for baseless excuses.

Some may say: "I work two jobs, and I am tired by the end of the day" ... how about you reprioritise your life, and you start your day with explosive sex with your spouse. It'll brighten up your day, and you might just have energy for more in the evening. Sometimes our lack of activity is what causes us to have chronic fatigue. The point is to avoid being comfortable in knowing what the problem is without pursuing a solution. If you have to change your diet to boost your energy levels, do that. Your marriage and your calling to be an instrument of joy in your spouse's life is more important than staying in that comfort zone.

1. An argument is not reason enough to forgo sex.

We were 20 days into the challenge when we had a blow-out moments before '*the act*'. I had to get something off my chest, and I did. The mood was sour for a bit, but the conversation was had. We slowly picked ourselves up and went into the act... I must say it was one of the hottest throughout the streak. Not only this, but the day after was super stunning. I realised that 'make-up sex' is incredibly passionate. But I also learnt that our arguments are just a fierce face behind which lies a yearning for each other. In truth, most of our arguments are born out of a petty expression of our need for attention. Evaluate your own arguments, and you will realise that all you want is your spouse to pay more attention to you. This can be achieved via a simpler route of mature conversation. But say you do get into an argument, let not that argument be a hindrance. In our experience on Day 20, I learnt that it is possible to enjoy sex in the midst of trouble.

Another example of this is Day 14; it was incredible. So incredible that 'someone' told 'someone' they're "amazing." The most interesting part was also the fact that this came off the back of a disagreement we had in the dining room. What made it all interesting is how we both glanced over our differences and jumped straight into 'The Act' and parked the disagreement and its resolution till after the act. What I learnt from this is that we often use sex as a reward for good behaviour, similar to the carrot and stick analogy above- you get it when you've been a good boy/girl, and you don't get it if you've been bad. I don't judge anyone who behaves like this because the idea of action and reward is coded into us. That's why we struggle so much with grace, because nothing is required from us, yet we gain much more than words can express. However, I encourage you to break from this cycle, and try something different. Whatever your reasons for not 'giving it to him/her' in the past, how about you 'give it' despite those reasons and see what happens.

If I were to advise anyone keen on trying the challenge, I would begin by warning that that some days are functional, the sex almost feels reduced to nothing but the continuation of the streak. Fret-not, I was also there during the streak. But what I learnt, albeit in hindsight, was that each sexual encounter was keeping the flame alive and serving as a preparation for the next. When I saw each sexual encounter as an addition to a wider story of the streak, it became less of a chore and more of a pleasure. Perhaps this can be extrapolated to your life in general. If you are to view each sexual encounter as a piece of a big puzzle of your experiences in sex with your spouse, it becomes less about the sex for the sake of the sex, but sex for the sake of the relationship and sex life. Realise that most of us are in pursuit of a better sex

life not a better sexual **encounter,** but a sex life is built with multiple sexual encounters.

I enjoyed the challenge. I recognise that there were moments that I had to condition my mind and steer it away from doing it for the sake of the streak. I learnt quite a bit about myself, including the fact that challenges really get my *A-game* out. I tend to be more consistent when there is structure around doing anything. I also learnt that my wife and I can band together to tackle any challenge, including the one of making a habit to connect both physically and emotionally, which is the biggest takeaway for me. I felt that we connected more emotionally and over the course of our challenge, we rarely got into heated arguments. Disagreements were there, but they never hindered us from doing life together.

Speaking to my wife about the streak, she noted how having a challenge like this made her more conscious of having sex regularly. She noted how instantly the thought of sex crossed her mind each morning. And since sex is a thing of the mind, she was constantly simmering and ready for it. I on the other hand was more than excited to be part of this tango. I was constantly aware of my need to conserve energy in order to be able to partake in this wonderful streak. We found ourselves planning activities around our daily romp (or romps) rather than having it the other way round.

Prior to the challenge, we had had a wish of being 'in the act' everyday, at least once. After 21 days, Day 22 was revealing. Lying in bed with my wife for our usual chat, she confessed that sometimes we wish for things that we realistically cannot understand or cope with. Having sex daily with the same oomph was a mammoth task, especially with being a parent, dealing with house chores and juggling a career. Physically, this required enough to make sex undesirable. But for so long we had been chastising ourselves for not 'doing it' daily. Don't get me wrong, we had a steady flow, just not a daily-bread kind. The lesson for me was appreciating what we had before being critical of it by comparing to a pie in the sky idea that you have sex daily. It may work for some couples given their situation, but doing the challenge during one of the busiest months of the year was quite a revelation. I was quite grateful that there were natural barriers to daily sex (i.e., periods, pregnancy and childbirth, illness, etc...). Most men would bite the hand off of someone who offered them sex daily. But the truth of having sex daily, often doing it multiple times a day is quite taxing. Especially if you're the kind that really throws down when they're in the act. In this sense, there is truth in the warning "be careful what you wish for [you might just _get it_]" ... How about you try the challenge and let me know your thoughts? Perhaps you will make more realisations than we did. I would like to read about your experience. Email me, I will appreciate it greatly.

The round-up

Much of what is discussed above relates to communication in some way. Communication, therefore, is key to a successful sex life and marriage by extension. In fact, the quality of your communication with your spouse is directly correlated to the quality of your marriage and your sex life. I would suggest that you address any issue in your marriage by examining the quality of your conversations (i.e., how frequent are they? How long do they last? Are they arguments or conversation, etc...)? The Love languages book[46] is a great resource in fixing communication. I would also add _His Needs, Her Needs_[47] because much of what we communicate is from the vantage point of our needs. Men tend to demand more sex because it is a need for us. Women tend to cry out for intimate conversation because it's one of their needs. The mismatch comes with us thinking that our needs are the needs of our spouses, i.e., just because my foremost need is sex, my wife needs it the same way too.

These ideas are geared toward keeping the flames of attraction and sexual intimacy burning hot. This requires consistent and intentional action, but consistency and intentionality shouldn't become a chore or a checklist. This is what we learnt during our 30-day sex challenge; enjoying sex is the point of it all. More so, enjoying a wonderful relationship.

P.S. If you're wondering how we sustained sex for 30 days, this was the post-partum season where periods were nowhere to be seen... What a blessing this is #wink.

Chapter 10: Miscellaneous

This chapter begins the final section of this book. After covering the areas discussed in the previous chapters, I would like to examine ideas/points that seem uncorrelated, but all relate to sex. This is why I have called it the *Miscellaneous* chapter, because of the diversity of the discussion points here. I would also like to caution you with the words that in staying with the spirit of this book, we will not be going on a full expository journey. Rather, we will extract from each area of discussion the key ideas relevant for married sex among Christian couples. Miscellaneous should not be mistaken for irrelevant or meaningless in the context of this text, however, there is no direct relationship between each sub-heading when compared to the next but combined, they contribute positively to a successful sex life between a married couple.

In writing this section of this book, my prayer is that the contents provoke you to action, and that the Holy Spirit assists you in your unique circumstances pertaining to each sub-section.

The Law of Attraction

Attraction plays a huge role in sex. If sex is a mind game, then attraction is at the heart of a winning game-plan. We see this littered all across our natural environment, especially among animals. Watch any animal show where mating season is covered. What you will note is that these animals will go all out to impress and attract a mate. For them, it is a matter of survival and continuing their kind, for us, it is a bit different but the value attracting and **keeping your spouse attracted to you** cannot be overstated.

The words in bold are the area where we struggle. During our season of courtship/ dating, call it what you will, we invest much time in preparing ourselves to appear in front of our beloved. As the years go by, we mind ourselves less and less. Sure, our tastes change over time, and with communication we can stay abreast with these but the attitude of pursuing attractiveness for our spouse should be up there in our priority list. Attractive takes different meaning for different people, so find out what your spouse's dials are. Brush up on that sense of style you had back then or pick up that dance class for you to get in shape again.

What I have noted in my own marriage, my wife seems to be fired up by seeing me workout, so I have opted to have the gym at home. The idea that she is attracted to my being in the act of working out and pursuing a healthy lifestyle is amazing to me. She doesn't care much about the finished article as she does with seeing me pursue it.

Some quick hits on the attraction front... Focus on hygiene. I don't think there is a man out there who would be willing to *go down* on an unhygienic wife and vice-versa. So, before you start accusing your spouse of a lack of spontaneity, examine yourself. My personal tip is to shower once a day at minimum, or you can do it like me and take a shower in the morning and evening. This ensures that you are likely to have that evening romp on a clean slate. More on hygiene in Chapter 7 *Oral Sex.*

Sexual Compatibility (Hot love = Hot Sex)

We're not in sync anymore, she complained. She's not the woman I married; he protests. We're no longer compatible.... All these are things people say when referring to that flaming attraction they had with each other where they seemed to be in lockstep with each other. The space where they finish each other's sentences, think the same thoughts and sing the same songs even when they are in different rooms. What kills this synchrony over time?

A friend of mine once explained that there are types of 'love' in marriage. There is the love of entry, which is the love you feel and have at the start of your relationship, that love that prompts you to desire being by your spouse's side all the time, staring into his or her eyes endlessly. Then there is the love of staying in marriage, this is the love that is less driven by feelings but the kind that keeps you together through the storms. It is mature and doesn't seem quite like the love of old. It is not an admission of defeat to the coldness of familiarity, but the recognition of a maturing relationship. It is this love that has an inexplicable way of making you and keeping you compatible.

Our ideas of sex, what it is and how it should be in a marriage are often fantastical. We expect hot sex but fail to love our spouses outside the bedroom. I will say this again, the quality of your sex life is directly correlated to the quality of your relationship. So, if 'HOTT SEXX' is what you seek, I challenge you to start pursuing 'HOTT LURRRRVVV'... Seek to serve your spouse in the ways that matter to them and speak their language of love. The reciprocal nature of this mystery called marriage is that when you do this you are likely to get what you need and a lot more of what you think you want less strenuously.

Lasting Longer in Bed (See Chapter 5)

Again, our popular culture teaches us that lasting long in bed is the holy grail of sexual experiences. While the ability to last long in bed for men is a great positive, lasting long while your spouse has had enough can leave you unsatisfied. On the other hand, the ideal of lasting long being central to great sex can cheat you of some steamy quickies that are such a blessing, Amen!

Stamina also depends on energy levels. These will spike and dip over the course of the day depending on our eating, level of exertion and also depending on our vocation, for example, people who do labour-intensive work are likely to see a dip in their energy levels and this may affect their performance in the sack. Another example is the correlation between high-stress seasons at work with lower to no sex drive. In view of these, it is clear that lasting longer as an ideal is both arbitrary and purports sexual enjoyment as an experience isolated to how long the sexual act lasts.

Rather than seeking to last longer, how about you focus on delivering pleasure to each other as a couple- whatever that may mean for you, but I am willing to put my reputation on the line and say that a pleasurable sexual experience is dependent on much more than the time it takes.

Another pro-tip is to linger on the foreplay. Much of the narrative about lasting longer revolves around vaginal penetration using the penis. Spice things up a bit, and last longer in foreplay- you'll thank me.

Okay, I promise this is the final word on lasting longer. Often, what makes most men capitulate during sex is that they are too self-conscious, and not in a good way. Too much mental energy is employed in trying to keep from 'exploding' that you miss being in the moment. Slow down, breathe and focus on enjoying the beautiful moment you're having with your wife. This goes for women as well, train your mind to be present in the moment with your husband. Don't be thinking about undone chores and your endless to-do list for the day ahead. Sex is to be enjoyed, so enjoy it.

Exercise for Sexercise

At a time before my wife and I got married, she had attended a bridal shower where one of the speakers advised the bride-to-be to *exercise for sexercise*. The phrase has stuck with me since. The importance of exercise was well and truly established in my mind during our 30-day sex challenge in April 2023.

I remember fatigue setting in about a third of the way into the challenge[48]. The excitement of having sex wore off as the reality of the effort it required dawned on me. At the time, I had been away from exercise for a while and had just started getting back. To say we were unfit is quite generous. Yes, the desire and urge were there, but the body was not very kind. My wife cried about her knees, my back did some popping, and we both broke into streams of sweat just moments after starting. The fact is sex is an exercise that demands exercise. (Sexercise)

Exercise is a key component to overall wellbeing. It reduces stress, increases resistance to illness and boosts our psychological state of being. Exercise also boosts our sexual performance. From our ability to hold complex sex positions to our stamina, exercise increases our enjoyment of sex and ensures that we are able to enjoy this gift much longer in life. I am one of those who wants to be going on romps late into my 70s, so longevity is a priority for me (pun unintended, or maybe not #wink).

Exercise alone is not enough though, as one has to also watch what they eat. My brother in-law is a qualified personal trainer, and he always tells me- 'S'bu, you can't out-train a bad diet' and I am afraid he's right. We are what we eat, and so feeding our body with the nutrients it needs is essential for our health and our sexual health.

I am not an authority in dietetics nor exercise, but what has worked for me, and my wife is this:

- **Reducing Sugar, Oil and Salt** (S.O.S)

- **Eating more vegetables and fruit**, especially fruits with lower fructose and leafy green veggies.

- **Reducing or even cutting out meat**... We aim for no more than 20% of meat in our meals per week. The focus is on reducing red meat.

- **Exercise at least 4 times a week** for about 30-45 minutes. Weight training is essential, but for us men the upside is even better as we age. I usually aim for 5 sessions- 2 cardio and 3 weight training.

- **Sleeping well**; Unsurprisingly, sex contributes to better sleep. But exercise has been shown to improve the quality of our sleep. In fact, the two work together. What happens when we sleep? Our body replenishes itself; our brain gets to rest, and our body heals itself. It's amazing. So quit bragging about how you never sleep, and your hustling... Sleep better.

- **Drinking at least 2 litres of water daily**. This tends to happen automatically when you exercise. In the early day of my marriage, a friend of mine encouraged me to encourage my wife to drink more water, it's supposedly a great way to minimise vaginal odour. There is no scientific evidence I can share with you on this, but knowing my friend, he has a wealth of traditional knowledge that has been passed down generations. And there is no harm in trying it. Another aspect of this is the quantity of water. I say 2 litres because that is what I aim for. There are other metrics out there like drinking half your body weight in ounces, and things like that. The problem is not the quantity, the problem is that you're likely going to focus on how much you should drink and not the actual drinking of water. Do the right thing. Lastly, avoid flavouring the water or thinking tea suffices as it is largely water. The 2 litres I speak of here is just clear water, no additives. Lastly, something I have tried to live by for many years now- first thing in your mouth when you wake up is a glass/cup of water, preferably warm. Last thing in your mouth should be the same, preferably warm also.

The above tips are what work for us, you can use them as inspiration and tailor them to your specific preferences. But make a start, if you haven't already. You will thank me later. Another fun part about exercising is seeing the transformation in your body, and the way your spouse will appreciate a sexier you. I love it.

There's No Abstinence in Marriage

Our traditional wedding vows have a line that we often glance over; 'In sickness and in health.' It is a phrase we utter with a smile, but the reality of it may not be so smiley. The truth of living out these words is much more costly than the ease of uttering them. If you are living through a season of caring for an ailing spouse, or have the experience of doing so, you would agree with me. Coming to the realisation that your entire life is now consumed with ministering care to them, sometimes at the expense of caring for yourself is a hard pill to swallow. The other aspect of this may be the ailing spouse's resistance to receiving such care, especially men and those of us who take great pleasure in doing things for ourselves. During these times, sex is not even a secondary issue, it is usually the last thing on our minds. Sadly, our bodies don't always align with the situation.

The thing with sex is that it is a multi-pack of things. It is a means of release for some, connection for others, and everything in-between. Depending on what you need at that moment, sex could be the *gateway* to the answer. For instance, a spouse who has received news of the passing of a dear parent, may relish at the opportunity of sexual connection as a means of reassuring them that they are still alive in **this** relationship and that they are loved, still (written with experience). The problem is that you may need this, but your partner is the one who's ill and cannot be there for you in that way, in that moment.

This requires you to draw from your experience as a single person, where you may have had the opportunity to, but you stayed away from extra-marital sex[49].

What I am saying is that abstinence doesn't end at the altar. In fact, you are more likely to get sexual advances, or derivatives of this when you are married. It is no coincidence; the enemy wants to destroy the nuclear family using our sexuality. Sexuality is sacred, hence the LGBTQIA+ is such a force, because the nuclear family and God-ordained view of sexuality threatens the kingdom of darkness. I have a couple of married friends and the gents always tell me about their experiences with women throwing themselves at them. My response is always to show them the enemy's game-plan, steal (from), kill (your marriage) and destroy (your marriage and life). So, if you expect you abstinence to end at the altar, what happens when your spouse is ill, away on business...?

Going a day without sex was unimaginable for me in my premarital stage. I always chatted with my then unmarried friends as we all agreed that sex would be our *daily bread* and that we hope God would give us spouses who would be of similar inclination. We always assumed that there's no abstinence in marriage, at least between a man and his wife. Alas! We were wrong, because life is not linear, and we go through different seasons. So, when life throws you lemons- these are situations when sex is practically (or even physically) not possible, what do you do? What happens when your spouse is ill, away on business?

Just over a year into our marriage, my wife had to go for a surgery which meant that sex was off the table for at least 2 months. Now, for the seasoned couple who have been married for many years, it is not an abominable thought. For me, it was going to be a mammoth task. In hindsight, I am grateful for that season, because I found ways of expressing my love to my wife that weren't sexual. I met her needs emotionally through encouragement, I met them physically by taking care of her during the process of healing, and we also had some bonus moments when I stepped in to help her with *bodily functions* that were previously embarrassing for her to share. It was a great time for deepening our relationship.

For the spouse who's away on business, some interesting ideas that leverage the power of technology have come to light. We covered sexting in chapter 9 when we went through *Some Ideas on Sex*. But there are other ways that you can keep the spark alive even when you're apart. Personally, I am not a fan of going on video with my wife and masturbating (more on this in the section on masturbating). I am also not so inclined to send nudes to my wife, nor is she. This is down to personal preference because our reasons are over safety on the internet. I've heard stories of people sending nudes and intimate messages to WhatsApp groups thinking they were messaging their spouse (#yikes). How are the group members ever going to get the image of the lady pastor in a G-string out of their minds...? But it may not be as deep for you and your spouse, you could be using a VPN and using a separate chat application specifically for your sexting to minimise the risk of leaks. The point is, there are ways around it and it is an option. From a biblical standpoint, I am yet to read a passage that prohibits this kind of fun between husband and wife.

Sex during trying times

Death is a tragedy. One that saps the life out of you and cripples your desire for anything and everything. Tragedy has struck 4 times in 18 months at our home. My two cousin-brothers, my dad and uncle. All gone, leaving me and my family with so many questions that remain unanswered to date. What has also been apparent in those times of loss is my lack of appetite and a lack of interest in work, play and everything in-between. During these times, sex was never off the table. But for some, it may be that the idea of sex irks them.

I've learnt that there are far more benefits to sexual connection than we care to think about. It has been my experience that the closeness that comes with sex plays a vital role in the healing process of myself and my wife. It is in these times where one feels the closeness and the oneness lightening their load as they go through a tough time.

Now, there may be some bothersome questions that spring into your mind: where I get the appetite from, or where do we get the privacy and the time to even give this a try. But have you stopped and wondered why it feels so natural to think that sex is off the table when you go through tragedies like losing a loved one. This is because of our beliefs that we ought to be consumed by the situations we face; just because I lost someone I love doesn't mean I need to step back from the people that remain and the relationships I have. In fact, I need them more than before. Another issue is that most people probably don't think this way because they have never considered it to be a possibility. My suggestion- have the conversation with your spouse and see what they have to say about it. You may be surprised to think that you are giving each other space you don't need because you're making well-intentioned assumptions that don't serve you well.

Even after this talk I'm suggesting, if you find that having sex in such circumstances is not your cup of tea, don't drink it. But be careful not to ridicule it simply because it's not something you fancy... if that is the only reason, it is not reason enough.

A final word on days like these (i.e., tragedy, loss in the family, illness, etc...): these are generally sex-free days for most people... What to do when sex is not possible? For whatever reason? I have a few tips:

First, keep the spark alive. Keeping the spark alive requires that you communicate love in other ways. Help in the kitchen always does it for most women. Or a hot bath after a long day. All this doesn't have to end up being sex. But it can be foreplay and help keep your spouse simmering for your next sexual romp.

Contraceptives

Our experience with these has been quite a revelation. My thanks go to my wife for allowing me to share this story. I hope that it will somehow be a ministry of hers to educate women about the reality of using contraceptives.

Ahead of our marriage, we went to a family planning clinic, ironically, it was one that also provides abortion services. It is a wonder that one would receive pro-life medical services from a place that performs procedures such as abortion. I can remember the sadness and heaviness I felt going into that place and seeing the guilt on some of the people's faces. I remember one 'couple' who weren't married as the guy was trying to reason with the girl about what was about to happen.

Despite all this, we went ahead with having an IUCD fitted into my wife. In hindsight, I am filled with such regret and shame that I was 'supporting my wife' in having a device fitted in her that had the potential of ruining her dreams of becoming a mother. Forget how the stats say it is 98% safe, what if we were part of the 2%? That's the downside of having stats spat at you by 'medical professionals'- they always tend to favour what the doctor wants to do to you, i.e., they will tell you the stat if it supports their recommendations... it's confirmation bias on another level. Respect to all medical professionals, it is not their fault that people are pumped with pharmaceuticals. Anyways, my wife would later experience terrible pains, and have the 'ultra-safe' IUCD pulled out- ouch, which also came with its troubles. In came the pill, and that came with a glorious 12-months plus of depression, vaginal dryness and hormonal roller coasters. To say my wife was in the pits during this time doesn't do her condition justice. It culminated in a random cist on her tailbone that required surgery, which made her unable to wash herself for two-months. This is when we decided to go old school. But what a way to change contraceptives, from IUCD, to the pill, to abstinence in marriage.

You read that right, at some point we cycle counted and avoided sex. Until we began making use of protection, which is not the same thing. My advice is that you remember that all actions have consequences, so consider the consequences of the course of action you take concerning contraceptives. Be very discerning when reading anything about them. If you wanted my verdict, stay away from them.

It doesn't always have to end in sex

When was the last time you gave your spouse a steamy kiss for no reason other than the fact that you love them? Have you ever? If your answer is either *'never'* or *'not in a long time'*, consider giving it a try and seeing what the result is like? Also consider why you haven't in a while or you've never. What will often come to light will lead to a deeper conversation? Perhaps there has been a break in the relationship, or you're not too keen to do so on the basis of hygiene. Whatever the reason, it's rarely based on dislike for your spouse or the act of kissing.

Sometimes, the hindrance is your perception of yourself and/or your spouse and what they are like as a person. Kissing without reason is usually associated with being overly romantic and showy. Some people don't consider themselves romantics, and so the idea of kissing for little to no reason is just farfetched for them. But give it a try, you'll never know whether you like it until you try.

However, the idea of kissing should not always be about it leading to sex. The problem with this behaviour of "kiss = sex" is that it demeans an affectionate gesture to a mating call. Not that mating calls are lesser than, but you want to be able to show affection without it leading to or signalling a call to sex.

I remember a men's meeting we had at church where one of the pastors was talking about how he and his wife don't hold hands [in public]. Admittedly, they don't call each other pet names either. He tells the story of how in the early days of his marriage, he tried holding his wife's hand and she refused because she said it would be inappropriate to hold hands in front of elderly people. As a result, the handholding was shelved until she tried holding his hand much later in their marriage, which he responds to with a sense of feeling weird and uneasy because it has become unusual. This story is not a sad one, because the people in it have a happy and fulfilled marriage, one in which they have various other ways in which they show affection. The lesson is that kissing and public displays of affection in the conventional and romanticised way are good, but their absence does not signal a lack of affection because there are other ways to show it, just as long as it is something that works for both partners. Lastly, I would like to qualify the story of the 'handholding' couple; they were married in the mid 1980's and they happened to have grown up in an African (IsiZulu) culture, where love and affection are associated with respect and honour, rather than kissing and handholding. Your context can be different, which means your definition of affection is likely to differ from others and have its origins in your culture. The chief aim of affectionate gestures should not be a means to sex, but a medium of communicating love, especially to the spouse that needs that as a love language they respond well to[50].

You don't have to be a "romantic" to have great sex

The idea of love these days is 'chocolates and flowers', not self-sacrifice and service. Contrast what we think love is and what people though love was a century ago, and you'll realise that our idea of love has become more romanticised. We've even mixed democracy and feminist undertones into what we believe love should be [in marriage]. It's no surprise then, that a lot of men would feel like they don't live up to the standard because they're not romantics. For some, they are likely to put on a false pretence at the start of a relationship just to woo their spouse and have that behaviour fade out over time. It's also unsurprising that many relationships breakdown within a few years after marriage, because in time the façade clears up and the real personalities show.

When my wife and I courted, I refused to buy flowers for her because I knew that I couldn't keep-up with the trend financially. I also felt like it wasn't a sustainable way of expressing love at the time. Later, I would buy her flowers and chocolate and have it personally delivered to her at work. This grand gesture earned me so many 'points'. But this gesture doesn't mean anything if I fail to express love in the seemingly little things; the way I treat her daily, my speech, what I do to help around the house, and being there to do life with her, and doing things for her. The seemingly little things are what matter most, so that being a romantic in the typical sense is not necessary for you to have a great relationship nor a great sex life. Marriage is about the satisfaction of each other's needs. My wife may **want** the experience of personally delivered flowers and chocolates, but she **needs** to be treated well daily. This is not to disregard the value of "romantic" gestures, but to advocate for them being coupled with consistent expression of love in ways that matter most to your spouse.[51] It is no use lavishing your spouse with gifts when their needs aren't being met... Your marriage cannot survive on a bad diet. Just like eating tons of dessert and skipping the veggies is a bad diet that will land you in hospital, a lot of one thing will land your marriage in *matrimonial hospital* even to the point of death. None of us want to be in ailing marriages, so we ought to do the right thing; take care of each other's needs emotionally, spiritually, intellectually and physically.

Sex When You're Sick

I had the flu, and my wife took care of all my needs except for one- sex. I tried to approach her as was custom in our house, when she told me what I needed was rest, not sex. It made me think; should you be having sex when you're sick? Or better, should you do it when you don't feel like it?

The first question is a matter of desire and possibility. The latter is a matter of duty. Scripture paints us a picture of physical duty to each other. It says the wife does not have authority over her body, but the husband does. Similarly, the husband does not have authority over his own body, but the wife does (1 Corinthians 7:4). The verse prior to this one speaks of each spouse rendering due service to the other sexually. We see here that satisfying our spouse's sexual needs is a command, and we respond to this command dutifully with obedience.

We can debate this, but when I am attune to the idea that my body belongs to my wife, I understand that I cannot treat it anyhow because it doesn't belong to me. I also understand that I cannot rightfully withhold it from her because it is hers. Likewise, if she adopts the same mentality, we stop seeing sex as a duty and see it more like an act of loving service to the other. I give my wife the best version of my body possible because I love her. I want her to get the best value from my body as far as sex is concerned so I guard it with all I have. I keep it from harm, and I keep it active so it can perform as well as it should when she needs it. This is not an isolated doctrine in the bible, we are all created to serve others. When God gives us blessings, we get them so we can be a blessing to others. If we don't use them to bless others, we are misusing them.

The second aspect of my initial question was a matter of desire and possibility. Some ailments make it difficult to perform sexually. This is why living clean and eating clean is important, because it reduced your risk of contracting diseases that will make it difficult for you to enjoy physical activity including sex. Another aspect of this second part is that of desire. When we're ill, we lose our appetite for food and other things we would ordinary jump at the opportunity of doing. Sex may or may not be one of these, and again this is something worth considering. If I were a third party, advising my wife in the moment I approached her for sex while I had the flu, I would advise her to give it a try. Especially because I got the flu from her.

So sex should never be taken off the menu because you're sick, if the desire and possibility is there, it is worth trying.

Getting Wet

I've probably said this multiple times in this book- you can't float a boat on dry land. You cannot enjoy sex comfortably without the genitalia getting moist enough to do so. This requires foreplay and patience. What tends to be the view of sex is that both spouses respond to each other the same way. If anything, we are complete opposites. Men move from stimulation to arousal very quickly. It seems wrong to even consider the two as separate phases of sex. Women, on the other hand, tend to require consistent and intentional stimulation in order to get aroused and ready for sex.

The problem is that the ladies think guys know this intuitively, and so they expect us to take our time and maximise on foreplay. The guys, being quick to arousal think the same applies to the women- **it doesn't.** We're all different, so different that the stimulation required for one lady may be a fraction of that required for another. The key is to be patient with each other, understand that there are unique differences between the two sexes, and that they are beautiful in their own way.

You may wonder 'how' this is. Simple, when a man takes his time to get his lady fully aroused, he is effectively putting a massive deposit into the magnitude of her orgasm. Both the process and the outcome from this input are something to behold. And it gets better, when she has a satisfying orgasm, she is likely to want to try sex again. But because she just had a big orgasm, her body is better at getting to arousal much quicker and with less effort- more joy for both parties. For the women, knowing that you can fire up your husband's engine in an instant is somewhat empowering, you know that your body and the appearance of it is a gateway to your beloved's pleasure. In addition to this, you can get sex on-demand, so when you have the craving (as you may well do at certain parts of the month), you can count on this great gift of instant gratification.[52]

It is in your best interest to ensure that sex is enjoyed only when both parties are aroused and the genitals moist. There are various ques for this, but none better than visual and auditory ques, i.e., seeing and hearing feedback from your spouse. Another consideration that has been mentioned in this text is the use of lubricant. There are some who may have reservations with using anything down there... I'm not here to convince you that your reservations are wrong, but I am going to convince you to adopt a sense of measured adventure, give it a try and see if it works for you. Something fragrance-free and silicone-based usually does it.

Coming Together[53]

This is probably the 'holy grail' of sex, reaching orgasm simultaneously. By orgasm, I mean climaxing, which usually looks like ejaculation for men, and uncontrolled spasms of the genitals for women (and a release of sexual fluids). There are instances of non-ejaculatory orgasms for men, but that's beyond the scope of this text.

If you've had the misfortune of reading secular sexual content on this subject, you would have noticed that it is clouded with needless gravitas, almost as if to say it is for the elite. I have news for you- it is not. Coming together is nothing more than coordination. I will attempt to explain it without getting too technical.

Your body is designed to complement your spouse's body. Male genitals are stimulated by the pressure-glide motion of the vaginal walls during in-and-out strokes. As the woman reaches her climax, the walls tighten, increasing the pressure against the penis. This, accompanied with the flow of sexual fluids from both parties, but largely from the woman causing things to get super wet. Now wet/moist added to pressure is a sure way to get the man's penis extra stimulated and push him to climax. When these separate occurrences of spasmodic tightness and penile arousal and hardening happen simultaneously, both husband and wife experience what is called 'coming together'.

The coordination is in the communication. I bet you saw that coming (no pun intended). But you can only come together when you both know what it is like to be moments away from climax. You can hold back the release until you both are near enough. This coordination takes some practice, and one should not expect to get it right the first time. When you do it well, you will discover that there is no longer a need for you to say a word, you can just feel it as you connect to each other physically. It's beautiful. But be patient.

I Want More Sex (Satisfaction) *see Chapter 8: Keeping the Spark*

Alive

If I were to take a sample of married couples, say 100 couples, and ask them the simple question; 'would you like to have more sex'? Majority of them would say 'Yes', emphatically so. They would most probably answer this within the context of their own marriages and its status quo, but also for a reason other than past perceived lack.

We're so used to wanting more and better of everything. This is the human spirit, always seeking to be better than the former self. The variability of the reasons why many people want sex can easily keep you from seeing the truth. The reason why people want sex, and more of it is because it is the means of a deeper connection that transcends the physical realm into the spiritual. We all have a craving for such, but the question is how? How do we have more sex?

Having more sex depends on what 'more' means to you. 'More' is subjective, and usually an elusive concept that causes confusion. We all agree that more of anything is anything greater than the status quo. However, more does not define 'how much' more is expected/required.

Having more sex is an outcome of 3 things, viz. i.) Great communication, ii.) Intimacy, iii.) Well-aligned priorities. The first element is something that finds its way all over this book. Communication is the means by which we transport our ideas and emotions to others. Done right, within the context of 'having more sex', we can lovingly communicate this to our spouses in a way that they will understand and a way that will add value to our relationship. The issue is when we perceive a void in the area of sex and we resort to nagging and negative talk- it never works, it only worsens matters. More on communication is littered across this book, but to summarise things for you, it is the first and most foundational aspect to having more sex.

Secondly, the small matter of intimacy. Covered in more detail in Chapter 2 *Sex Happens in the Mind*, intimacy is much more than sex. Pursuing this all-important ingredient is a sure way to ramp up the frequency of the lovemaking in your marriage. Intimacy demands making time for each other, spending this time together with intention and direction. By intention, I mean doing much more than being in each other's presence. I make this example about assuming that watching a movie together with your husband/wife in cinema is the same as spending time with her; it is not. It is spending time with him/her in your presence, but not spending time **with them**. I also advocate spending time with direction, meaning that your intention must be supported by a noble goal. It should be more than getting into your spouse's pants, it should be about getting to know them deeply, so as to enrich your service to them. Remember, marriage is a covenant of satisfying needs. Meeting these needs requires knowing what they are and how they can be best met.[54]

Finally, more sex requires having well-aligned priorities. We live very busy lives; we claim to maximise outcomes from our inputs, yet we are the most frustrated generation in human history. Why? Misaligned priorities. In the context of sex, many people want more of it, but they also want to forego the ensuing two elements of communication and intimacy. You can't have it that way. The truth is that our current situations reflect our priorities. What you prioritise tends to consume much of your focus, in turn, it becomes who you are. An example is that of someone who lives a healthy lifestyle, their focus is on weight control and maintaining a strong body. They will eat, sleep and exercise accordingly. All this will show up in them having a strong, toned body.

Another excuse people give for their shipwrecked sexual lives and relationships is that they don't have time. I am sure it is the same excuse that they'd give when told to do the first two elements of this section- *I just don't have the time*. Unfortunately, neither do the people who have successful relationships and healthy sex lives. You see, we all have the same 24-hour days. The question is what do you do with yours? This is where well-aligned priorities come in. when your priorities align with your purpose and goals, then life becomes a more joyous experience with less stress and frustration. In fact, you can stomach the hard parts much more happily for the joy that lies before you. Getting back to our exercise example earlier, my experience is that greens and portion-control aren't the greatest of things, especially when there are so many temptations. But in order to reach your fitness goals, one has to mind their consumption. In a similar fashion, if your purpose/goal is a healthy marriage with a vibrant sex life, and your lived reality is something other than that, check your priorities. Perhaps you are spending too much time on things that don't contribute to you reaching your goal. Perhaps the TV/Cell phone/_____ is taking more time than the value it is giving back[55]. It is never too late to address this, if you're experiencing the results of misaligned priorities, a marriage lacking in communication and intimacy, make a start today, use some of the guidance provided in this book and may the Lord help you mend that relationship.

Lust Ends at the Alter

Marriage is sometimes viewed in the church as a hedge against lust. It is not. I am a witness to the fact that you get more 'attacks' to your purity after marriage than before. Much of the narrative about marrying for reasons of hedging against lust is based on the scripture which reads thus; "Now concerning the matters about which you wrote: "It is good for a man not to have sexual relations with a woman." **But because of the temptation to**

sexual immorality, each man should have his own wife and each woman her own husband (1 Corinthians 7:1-2 ESV)"

This is not to say that the objective of marriage is sex, rather that sex should be confined within the parameters of marriage. The result is that a husband and wife who serve each other sexually, help each other avoid fornication. This avoidance is not an aim, but the by-product of marriage. Further verses in this passage encourage spouses to give each other their conjugal rights and not deprive one another in this area.

If you struggle with lust, I am sorry to disappoint you; but marriage is not the answer. Jesus and His regenerating Spirit are. You see, if you are incapable of restraining yourself before marriage it is difficult to see how marriage will solve your issue. Picture it this way, your pursuit of purity does not end when you are married. As a single person, you guard against sexually sinning against God and your body (see 1 Corinthians 6:18, ESV). When you are married, your purity also involves avoidance of sin against your spouse. If I were the enemy, my target would be the married person, that way I hurt God, the sinner and their spouse. No wonder marriages are so challenged by sexual sin.

By this we see that marriage does not mean your battles with sexual temptation come to an end, the war becomes more aggressive. In my experience, some in the world claim that a married person is even more attractive because they can have a no-strings-attached relationship where they 'have a nice time' with the extra-marital partner and get back to their wife/husband. This is demonic rationality; the marriage bed is to remain pure and untainted. Praise God for His Spirit, which empowers us to prevail against the wiles of the enemy.

Sex during her period

I cannot explain the shock I got when I went into the bathroom and saw a red discolouration in the water of the toilet pan. My first reaction was to check if I had bled into the water. Even though I had not done anything yet. My second thought was to ask my wife 'What was happening'. I thought she was passing blood and that she was dying. This is back in the early days of our marriage when I did not know better.

The obvious reason, which may not be so obvious to us guys, is that my wife was on her period. She would later tell me this but had to reassure me several times to calm me down and quench my concerns. I grew up around mostly guys, so this was quite foreign. During this time, sex was out of the question. In fact, this had been a conversation we had prior to our marriage where I was the one who said sex was not to be enjoyed during her period. To be honest, I wasn't really sure why, I think I heard it from somewhere in a sermon talking about the Mosaic laws around women during their period. To my delight, my wife confirmed that she wasn't particularly in the mood for that, and that the thought of anything opposing the flow of blood down there irked her. Even more surprising was the knowledge that there are some who still engage in sex during this time. You must understand, I was still wet behind the ears in this thing. I did not know better.

Now to the matter of sex during a woman's menstrual cycle. The biblical standpoint is that it should not be done (See Leviticus 18:19, 20:18). Some believers claim that this was the Old Testament and that it ceased to have a faith-based significance when Christ died for us. Still, some also argue that these Levitical laws were for hygiene purposes, and that they are not spiritual in nature. My take is that the Levitical laws have spiritual authority over a believer, just like any other law. This is not to say I keep all Levitical laws, but to point out that these are God's laws for his people. I suppose this is why I need grace, because I don't keep them all. I will also admit that I have not given myself the time to study them in depth. In this instance, I suggest you make your own decision in communication with your spouse, just like I did.

Whether sex during your wife's period is okay with you or not okay with you, speak about it and come to a consensus. Better still, pray about it and consult with some seasoned men and women of God who will guide you from a spiritual standpoint. I would caution you though, from a medical standpoint. We may have advanced hygiene products, but we are still susceptible to blood-carried illnesses much the same as the Israelites all those centuries ago. If you're going to engage in sex during the wife's period, rather seek medical advice for your specific situation. But if it was for me, we would stay away from sex during this time. It is less complicated to understand and shields you from risk.

On a lighter note, we were months into our marriage and there was an ongoing prayer and fasting revival at our church. Days into this exercise, my mom walks towards my wife and asks: "Did you know that you are not supposed to..." while signalling her index finger going into an 'O' with her other hand... this has become our little symbol of sex. My wife, amused, would respond by confirming that we were aware and sticking to the rules.

Size Matters (double entendre)

Am I big enough for her? Am I satisfying my wife in bed? These are questions that cause anxiety for many guys in their marriage. Size matters are in the top 10 list of all secular sexual content. Should you be worried about how big you are? How important is it in satisfying your wife? Can you grow your size? These are interesting questions worth discussing.

First, you are not likely to grow the size of your penis past a certain age. Not without some major medical intervention that is likely to cost you more than you're willing to pay (financially and otherwise). The thing about penis sizes is that it is the same as bodies; they come in different shapes and sizes. Some are short and thick, others are long and thin, it's just all a biological differentiation issue. The thing that men often forget when they worry about the size of their penis is that the size of vaginas is also variable, and the fascinating thing is that regular sex with a person of a certain size will stretch the internal physiology of a woman's genitalia to fit that penis. This is so amazing, because in monogamous marriages where both spouses are faithful to each other, size should never be a problem.

Is it important in satisfying your wife? Well, the short answer is 'yes' and 'no'. If the husband had a 1 cm long penis, this would undoubtedly cause problems in using the penis as a device for sexual pleasure. So that is the 'yes' part of the response. On the other hand, size is a matter of reach, and this can be altered on the basis of sex positions. If you remember the contents of

Chapter 3 *Sex Positions*, you will remember that we dealt with the concept of Depth, Size and Stimulation (DSS). For some of the positions laid out in that chapter, you would note that the level of stimulation would change based on the position. An instance of this would be how doggy style would stimulate the G-spot more than the missionary position. So that stimulation does not depend entirely on size, though it is a factor, but more so on the position. Satisfying your wife is a matter of stimulation, and this can be achieved by optimising the position and not the size.

Lastly, the small matter of whether a man should worry about 'how big' they are? Frankly, nothing anyone says will cure your ailment on this one. This is all down to each person dealing with their own inner man. But I do have some truths that can aid in this. The first, is that 'big' or any synonymous word is relative. Something is big enough insofar as it is compared to something. So perhaps your struggle is not size, but comparison with others. The other truth is that there is always going to be someone bigger than you, so if you feel small about your size, you're actually feeling so on the basis of something you neither control nor have the power to change. The other sad truth is that there are some people who are 'blessed down south' but have very little know-how on sex. Just because your penis is the size of another man's arm doesn't make you a Sex Champion. The same applies for those who think lesser of their size, it only matters if you let it. My advice is getting in the habit of learning more about your spouse and how you can bring them pleasure with what you've got, rather than what you haven't. Remember, the first temptation was premised on lack, even though mankind had superabundance. So don't let Satan best you using that trick in your sex life.

To Porn or *not* to Porn?

Perhaps one of the most destructive industries there is out there. Porn destroys marriages, families and nations. At this point, it is not even an argument whether a Christian couple should consume porn (See *Chapter 4: Sexual Fantasies* for more).

The world will advocate for the use of porn as inspiration in terms of positions, and other sexual matters. But the key considerations about porn are laid out in chapter 4 and can be summarised thus:

- Porn is largely fuelled by trafficking and substance abuse. Many people who are participants in the porn industry are not doing so willingly. Some are victims of trafficking and others are held captive by addiction to drugs. Consuming this kind of content means you are a contributor to such an industry. One of the things that I always consider is how painful it felt when it hit home, perhaps it hasn't for you but consider those who have been victims and do your part in defunding this industry.
- Porn has the tendency of ruining one's ability to enjoy sex with their spouse. This is due to its rewiring your brain and desensitising you to the 'real thing'. If we are to be effective in serving our spouses sexual needs, we ought to get serious about keeping our minds clean.
- The biggest question to ask, when using porn, is whether or not your doing so serves the purpose of your sex life glorifying God or putting a smile on the devil's face? Chief among our aims with and in sex is to bring glory to God. By serving one another, we are serving God. Is porn addiction part of this service? It usually isn't.

If you're still not convinced about the horrors of porn use and insist on using motion-pictures for inspiration. Do a sex tape of you and your wife and keep that as a memory to revisit for inspiration. I personally don't see how this would be better than doing the deed, but it is an idea worth exploring

Masturbation in Marriage *are you serving yourself or your spouse?*

There is a lot of material in support of masturbation as a healthy way to reign in your passions. There are even rationalisations of it as a safe way to satisfy yourself sexually without hurting anyone's feelings or exposing yourself to any risk of STD's. All of these are true, but they are not truth.

You see the difference between truth and something being true is that the truth is unchanging. Whereas something that is true can change depending on the situation. I may go outside and say it is hot at 32 degrees Celsius. But a 15 degree drop in temperature may render my truth obsolete. The fact that I felt hot was true until the weather changed. On the other hand, the fact that the sun rises from the east is truth. Regardless of where you go, this is an established truth. Likewise, masturbation being healthy for you may be scientifically true, insofar as it relates to the release of sexual tension and avoidance of heartbreak and STD's. But the truth is that it is not inherently good.

Masturbation is a means of releasing sexual tension that involves a single person: the one masturbating. For men, this is sometimes an activity advocated for because it teaches how to 'edge' or control ejaculation. However, the fact that it is simulating sex but only involves one person indicates that there is a problem. Sex is about connection, therefore it requires two people for it to be what it was created to be.[56] Sex is also about serving the other, not yourself, which is something that any activity of masturbating never achieves, no matter how you can convince yourself otherwise. So masturbating is usually selfish, those who do it do so because they want to satisfy themselves.

Masturbating should not be found among saints. It desensitises you from the real thing, with some men struggling to enjoy sex with their wives unless they 'kick-start' themselves. Another subtle problem with masturbating is that it involves the casting of mental images, i.e., the feelings experienced physically are typically responses to mental images that are aided by pictures, memories or even porn. If one does masturbate without visual aids, this is usually an opening for unclean thinking. A married man may masturbate because it helps him somehow, but he becomes susceptible to imagining himself with that old flame of his, or any woman other than his wife.

Now there are instances where some may say that masturbating is a reasonable compromise, like the instance of long-distance relationships. My take is that people are celibate when they are unmarried (or so they should be), why can't they restrain themselves even when they are? I don't believe I should jump into a fire because I am feeling cold; there is a time, place and proper way of doing things, and masturbation never seems to be a positive for me.

Sex Toys, Sex Rooms and Sex Aids.... (Mmmmm)

We walked into one of our most frequented pharmacies (what's known as a drug store in some parts of the world). This is a family-oriented store that sells cosmetics, medication, supplements, and everything relating to self-care. To my surprise, I see a section on the 'supplements aisle' with a variety of sex toys. They are purposefully arranged at the top of the shelves, obviously because their targeted audience is likely to see them at this level. I was with my wife at the time, and I made a remark about how this particular store has finally joined the party. We went into a whole different conversation, but the substance of it was that of sex toys.

The big question is whether the bible permits the use of toys? Are Christians even supposed to have sex rooms or use sex aids. I don't have a sex room. At the time of writing, I do not have a house big enough to enjoy this luxury. Sex toys aren't that big of a thing for me also. I guess my take on these things will be biased to my lived experience and preferences.

The short answer to the question of whether Christian couples should use sex toys, aids and have sex rooms is **it depends.** The first issue with sex toys and aids is the risk of dependence. The second issue with these is that introducing them too early into your journey may mean forgoing some valuable experience with getting creative. The other issue is the all-important question of whether or not your actions glorify God.

The idea of our sex glorifying God may seem wild. But believe me when I say God is glorified when we enjoy a healthy and vibrant sex life in marriage. The concept of glorifying God refers to doing stuff that brings Glory to His name. Glory is what ensues winning; athletes are glorified (i.e. rewarded with

CRASH COURSE ON SEX FOR CHRISTIAN COUPLES

medals and trophies) when they obtain victory. Being created by God and marriage being His institution, sex in a Godly marriage brings Him Glory (i.e. He gets the credit for His creation performing as He intended).What form this takes from one couple to the next may differ, but the overarching principle is that God is glorified when we walk in His law. And His law is governed by love. So, when we enjoy sex with our spouses and we do so in love and service to the other, this brings honour to God's name and His name is glorified.

The other issue is that of sex toys being overwhelming, especially when you're just starting out in marriage. You still need to get comfortable with the idea of being totally naked in the presence of someone you've not had to show your nakedness to. Then they bring in this device you plan on using to supposedly pleasure them? Absurd! Take it easy on the toys, and trying anything new. Just remember that proper communication is very important in this regard. If, after getting comfortable and *au fait* with the idea of sex and you still want to introduce a particular toy... talk about it. Our rule of thumb is that we don't do anything unless we both agree to it. If one of you doesn't want to use toys, then no toys should be used.

Chapter 11: Sex for New Parents

Our Bundle(s) of Joy

Children are undoubtedly a gift from God. They bring so much joy to our lives and they give us first-hand teachings on what it is to be a child of God. During the writing process of this book, I became a parent to our first child, Samkele Sibusiso Thabethe, Jr. The road to his arrival was so exciting, holding him for the first time was exciting, and even looking at his innocent face for the first time was a wonderful feeling. I could not believe that I had an entire human being who depended solely on me and my wife for his survival, it just clarified so much about my own relationship to God.

Anyways, the excitement ended when he began crying in the night, especially when the doctors had given the *green light* for my wife and I to 'get busy' again[57]. This can be a frustrating experience, one which I had heard of from a few of my married friends. One of them had related a story when both he and his wife were so keen to get their sex freaks on, but their lovely bundle toddler would not go to bed... talk about blocking.

So how do you manage your sex life in the midst of distractions, demanding commitments or a schedule that is simply too busy for you to even think of sex? Not to add the responsibility of being a parent? Sharing some insights and possibly answering these questions is the purpose of this chapter. Similar to marriage and sex, parenthood is a journey we enter into with very little training, perhaps it would be wise to consider the idea of a crash course on parenting someday, God willing. For now, let's focus on the matter at hand-sex and being a parent. Before we do, a word of caution to those long-past their days of parenting infants and toddlers, consider the ideas presented here. The contents may easily and readily be transferred to other areas of our lives that tend to require our attention[58].

Below are some tips that I have seen to be helpful in my own marriage, and perhaps you can glean a thing or two from them for yours.

Take the wins

We have so much negative energy in the world today. Watch the news for half an hour and you'll be dizzied by the negative reporting out there. Social media is no different. Conversations with colleagues at work, or any other platform where people connect- all negative, at least for the most part. Unfortunately, this is a mind-set that flows into our homes.

If we are asked on how well we are doing in balancing things as a parent and a spouse, the response would go something like: "We're trying, but it is hard" or "I'm struggling, I just hope we are doing it right"... your responses might be even tougher... but the point is made. The issue is that we are so attune to detecting the stuff that isn't going right, that we do not discern when we are doing right. Even if we do, we don't give ourselves credit for it[59].

This is less about sex and more about our mentality. Appreciate the good you are doing and resolve to improve on the other things. Typically, when we focus on the negatives, we end up wallowing in our own pity and that is no state-of-mind to be in, least of all if you are considering sex.

Teamwork makes the dream work

I suppose this may seem abstract to a lot of non-Christian readers, but working as a team in marriage is possible even with traditional gender roles. What I mean by this is that helping each other halves the work and doubles the satisfaction. If my wife takes an hour to prepare a meal for us single-handedly, we can do it in under an hour as a team. Replicate the same idea across multiple activities, and you have more time to spend doing other things, like having sex.

In my experience, one of the complaints my wife has had is that of being tired by the end of the day. So tired in fact, that I would find her fast asleep while sitting. Having a baby is physically exhausting, especially when the baby is breast-fed, because the mom cannot have the dad do the feeding. Breast-feeding also demands energy for two from a single source. This and the constant need to wake up and check if the baby is still alive; she's bound to be tired.

In situations like these, we need all the help we can get. To reduce her level of tiredness, I learnt to help where I can. Like giving the baby a bath, putting the laundry in the wash, hanging and getting it back in the house. An occasional breakfast is also wonderful, along with some cleaning. You'd be fascinated by how 'pregnancy brain' becomes less of a joke post-partum, my wife would forget to eat or even be so consumed that she doesn't get a chance to wash-up. Therefore, helping in any way possible reduces her to-do-list and avails time for some intimacy (which may or may not mean sex).

Although we're focused on sex in this book, we now understand that there is more to intimacy than sex. I learnt this after having our son. My wife and I went through so much being parents for the first time, so it was necessary for us to connect and to keep the connection alive through the journey. Sharing our struggles made them lighter to bear, and sharing our fears was also quite healing because we had each other. It's easy to struggle alone in the presence of a multitude of people, even in marriage, so connecting regularly is key.

A word for men

Women go through a lot during pregnancy all through delivery of their baby(ies) and even post-partum. I noticed that with my wife, the focus was so intense on our son that she somehow forgot to take care of herself. Hairstyling, looking fashionable, and even eating post-partum becomes a challenge. Emotions are also swinging here and there along with reduced sleep and the 24/7 worry about '*is my baby fine?*' took a toll on her physically. The best we can do in times like these is to support our wives. This may require that sex be 'taken off the table' while your wife recovers[60] (physically and mentally). You'd be surprised that some ladies take more time to adjust to the reality that sex is a possibility post-partum because their appetites swing to the nurture and care for their babies. So, it is most important that you **don't make assumptions but ask questions.** I heard someone say the way to hell is paved with good intentions. What I draw from this is that much of the destructive behaviours in relationships come from a good place, the problem is that we give the help we think we would need, and this is sometimes not the same as the help needed by those we're giving it to. A means of avoiding this is to ask- how can I help? Is what I am doing helping? How best can it serve you where you are right now? Etc...

It must be said that some of us like to think we're fine and can do all by ourselves. This is not how things should be done in a marriage. I'm usually guilty of this- I like doing things alone. I tend to think that things happen faster and better this way because I do exactly what I want, how I want it. Offering help to someone like my former self is difficult because it is met with **"I'm fine"**. The funny thing is that even when I need help, I would avoid asking because *I don't want to inconvenience my wife...* sadly, she doesn't appreciate this because it deprives her of ministering her love to me by means of service. The lesson here is to be willing to accept help, especially to mothers. You're not less of a mother if you let your husband (or anyone else) help you in caring for your baby. Just remember that your baby needs his/her mom to take care of herself so she can take care of him/her. Make a habit of taking some time off, even if it is a few hours. Just to recharge and centre yourself. You'd be amazed of how much you let yourself go in order to give to your baby. Make sure you're not pouring from an empty cup.

Skills transfer

In the industry that I work in, the ability to transfer skills from one area of expertise to another is a skill of its own. Transferring my skills of financial analysis to my personal life would make my lecturers swoon.

We often partition our lives to the point where financial experts find themselves in debt, or doctors suffering from ill-health. This dysfunction doesn't bode well for our sex lives, if you're a manager at work, how about you use some of those management skills to create an awesome sex life with your spouse. I don't mean that you should become a taskmaster to your spouse, but skills such as the management of resources (i.e. time, money, etc...) could come in handy in achieving great sex. What stands in the way of this is the notion that work, and life are to be kept separate.

Most people work in jobs they don't really like. It is then natural for them to want to forget their work and life lived there when they leave the workplace. But all experiences contain lessons that could be applicable elsewhere. Look for these skills that you rely upon at work, and see if you cannot do the same for your marriage. An example of this is how any job requires efficiency... that is, making the most of the least number of inputs. In marriage, this may look like putting your money to good use (see below examples). Collaboration is also something we practice in the workplace, where we leverage on each other's strengths to drive the team/organisation forward. Likewise, collaborate with your spouse in doing life together. I am reminded of how many a man will sit on the couch catching up on sports while the wife slaves away doing everything in the house, only for him to expect explosive sex later on. This is a dream, one that doesn't usually come true. I advocate for lending a hand where possible. This will maximise the time you can spend with your spouse as some of those chores will take less, plus you can spend time together doing something; it's a win-win.

My friend's wife said such profound words once, she said "You can't outsource spending time with your spouse". This is wisdom, first because it is true as it is. Second, because the negative implication is also true. Outsourcing is a useful tool to maximise the time you can spend with your spouse. I personally struggled to grasp this concept. I grew up in an environment that encouraged D.I.Y-ing and your abilities in this area are tied to your identity. I come from an environment where using a washing machine for laundry is considered being lazy. So outsourcing is hard for me, not to mention that it has financial implications, meaning that outsourcing makes me both lazy and wasteful. As I grow, I am learning that my time is infinitely more valuable than money or the risk of being branded lazy. Gradually, I want to outsource the stuff that take time out of my day and time away from the things I actually want to do. This could be your aim. For instance, getting a laundry service for the first few weeks post-partum is one way to reduce your to-do list while taking care of business. Another one is to get a food-delivery service; you'd be amazed how much pressure this takes off your shoulders. You neither have to worry about meals, or the buying of less than healthy meals. You can also consider outsourcing cleaning, gardening, car-washing, the list is endless. My rule though is this, what alternative use I can make with the time I am saving by outsourcing a particular activity. Usually, the answer to this is spending time with my family. You don't want to outsource an activity and spend the time 'saved' to something else other than family, or something that has a positive effect on you and your marriage.

Perfect doesn't exist

The *Perfection Syndrome* is one that I suffer from personally. The idea that everything should be perfect for it to be considered a success[61]. I somehow think that I should exercise 5 times a week, eat healthy every day, have sex 3 times daily, read a book, journal, work my 9-to-5 and still have energy to connect with friends and family, and write books, record a podcast, and upskill myself. If I miss one workout session, the entire week is *lost*- I have failed. This may seem amusing and absurd, but it is the reality of many among us. It is also the cause for depression and discontentment. If you're one of these, I have news for you- ***perfect doesn't exist.***

An hour spent in the gym is an hour of absence everywhere else. Sure, you can listen to a podcast while working out, tune into a sermon or connect with God while pumping iron. I do these things too, and I convince myself that I am being productive with my time, but my productivity is limited to a few activities at a given time. So, approaching your sex life with the perfectionist attitude is a terrible idea. There's no perfect in sex, it's a fact. We all need to accept that life happens, and you are not likely to have sex as often as you want, as good as you want it in the way you want it. This idea of on-demand sex doesn't exist.

In the context of sex and parenthood, the two are identical in the sense that they both require work, consistency and they are constantly a work-in-progress. What we can strive for is a good or even great sex life by being diligent and consistent in our efforts to create it. We can do this in many ways, including the ideas shared above and elsewhere in this book.

Create the environment for sex

Home alone, my wife and I, and our sleeping son lay peacefully in our beds. He's been down for over an hour and my wife starts looking at me with 'lustful' eyes, grabs me by the shirt and pulls me strongly toward her pouted lips. Things get heated very quickly and we move from simmering to blistering in seconds. Off go the clothes, and on our marks, we stand ready to exchange passionate lovemaking. This comes off the back of a successful *30-day streak*[62], the day is 30 + 1, and we're loving the moment. Then there is a shiver in the cot, and up rears a cute little head with the most wonderful baby yawns. He's awake- blocker[63]. A friend of mine had me forewarned about babies, he uses a soccer analogy and calls them the biggest and baddest defenders on the planet. The thought of his passionate warnings crossed my mind as the flames became ashes of a bitter *'it could have been'*. This is just one of the instances where babies have come in the way of sexual encounters between a couples. It takes real grace and love to look at a child caringly after that, I know, I have been there myself. Shortly after my misfortune, I rushed to put on my clothes and grab the little man out of his cot, and it was history. But the lesson here is to take every opportunity as it arises and to also leverage the power of planned sex. Plan around your child's sleeping schedule and ensure that you each have the energy to play. Nothing makes sex unfulfilling like a one-sided affair- you need to be in it together. Another quick note is the use of quickies; I have heard couples with older kids confess to sneaking away for a quick romp while the kids are occupied with something in the other room. The discreet nature of this 'mission' adds a dimension of adventure and much-needed playfulness in this tough world.

Developing a baby-free zone

Following the birth of our son, and purely out of excitement, much of our conversation with my wife have been about the baby. The different milestones, the various cute moments throughout the day. I've found myself wondering whether I was being seen by my wife or was I just the father of her baby. This may sound selfish, but I love my son, just not enough to have him swallow all the attention and have my wife focused completely on him. The other side of this coin was brought to light in the first time I took my wife for a date post-partum. She was so anxious to leave 'her baby' that I was near setting a timer for the amount of time we'd be away. In fact, we went to a fast-food joint that's 10 minutes from home just in case granny needed her to attend to the baby. As we pulled into the driveway, my wife flung the door open and rushed into the house to see if her baby was fine. He was good, and the drama died down after a while, but the lesson stuck with me- be patient with each other as you navigate the journey of parenthood, especially for the first time. You're both entering a new territory which brings a new dimension to your relationship. Further, note that each child born or adopted into your family is adding onto the dimensions spanned by your relationship. You become parents to another child, while still having to fulfil being spouses to each other and parents to your other children.

This calls for the development of baby-free zones. This does not have to be a geographical location, or a particular locus. Just resolve to avoid speaking at length about your kids in certain moments, like those dates you take periodically to reconnect with each other. In these moments, let the conversation be about you and your spouse. Nothing, or no one else. Simulate the conversations you had before marriage, where you shared your dreams, aspirations and how you make each other feel. When is the last time you were candid with your spouse about how you feel about them? All of these things are what brought you into marriage in the first place, they are good enough to sustain you through it also.

The need for a recharge

New mothers are thrust into an all-consuming season from the moment their baby arrives. The baby's existence depends on the mother. Naturally, her attention is always sought by the baby to feed, nappy changes, baths, and other cries only baby understands. Our experience was no different. From the moment our son was born, my wife's maternal instincts have been ever switched-on.

We were blessed to have no complications with the birth of our son; both mom and baby made it out of labour alive and well. He came at 3.431 KGS, 52cms at exactly 17h33 on the 10[th of] November 2022. Healthy lungs, ten toes and ten fingers- he has grown healthily since. For some, there is added stress with complications and baby being admitted to the NICU...

With childbirth being stressful enough, transitioning home and adjusting to life with a new member of the family requires measured effort and consideration. It is this setting where sex becomes the least of your concerns.

Very often, people view parenthood to be a replacement for their matrimonial responsibilities. The idea is that your responsibility as a parent outweighs your responsibility as a spouse. So much so that when I told people that were taking some time before we started having children, they were quick to remind me that having children changes everything, and that we would not have time for each other when babies enter the picture. Naturally, I am always opposed to the baseless views of the masses, this instance was no exception. I've always held to the belief that God's blessings do not come with sorrow, so if children are a blessing, there should not be sorrow.[64] Further, the blessing of parenthood is one we are given along with the capacity to handle.

My dad's legacy on isolation

My dad passed away just months before the birth of our son. He had been anticipating his arrival from the moment we broke the news of my wife's pregnancy. Leading up to his passing, he had had some stipulations[65] about his grandson. One of which was the fact that we would go into isolation for a month after he was born. No one was to visit us besides grandma and himself, of course. Initially, I thought this was dad being dad, always laying the law even when it was not necessary. I somehow decided to adhere to this stipulation and apply it. I initially said 3 months, this caused some tension between my wife and I, because she had a lot of people from her side of the family who were quite keen on seeing our baby, we ended up agreeing on a month.

It was after spending the month in isolation that we realised what wise stipulation this was. Post-partum is challenging enough for us to be entertaining guests. You are moving into a new season in life with so many moving parts, you don't know what is coming next nor do you have full control over your schedule. In our case, some days were spent recovering from a sleepless night. Not because our baby was overly fussy, but because we couldn't sleep without waking up to check on him every hour, just to see if he was still breathing and that we had not made a complete failure of ourselves as parents. But the substance of the lesson was that couples need time to adjust to having a new member of the family, without the interruptions that come with hosting people and having to look presentable for the masses.

What I also saw during this time was how we bonded over caring for our son. This may not have resulted in sex, ultimately, but it matured our relationship in a way that nothing else could; being co-parents to this wonderful baby boy. So, your isolation period may be more or less than this, but the key is to take time away from everything and just focus on your marriage and the baby(ies). You will find that these are moments you will cherish your whole life through and moments that will only make your relationship better.[66]

Routines, routines, routines

Let's be frank, having children around the house can get in the way of enjoying your sexual life with your spouse. But a further truth is that having anyone can get in the way of you two getting it on. What I often hear from couples implies that children are a distraction, they are not. I'm not trying to sound smart here, but children should not be viewed as a distraction from you enjoying your sex life with your spouse. The reasons that some may perceive children as a distraction is that they are awake in the moments when they want to *get it on*. Sure, your child may have the odd nights when they stay up late, especially during their infancy, but largely, they shouldn't. I'm submitting to you that some of the reasons why we pin the blame on children is because we are blind to the truth that it is our responsibility to train them in a way that allows us to enjoy our sex when we want to. The takeaway here is to plan well, and to implement routines that favour your plans.

A friend of mine shared with me that once, they sent their kids away to a relative during school holidays, and it was like they were experiencing the adventure of intimacy afresh. These and other tactics can be used to give you an opportunity to enjoy sex and each other's company without worry.

Besides sex, it may also be necessary for you to consider having outings, alone, without your children. Just the two of you. Get a babysitter, take a short 2 - 6-hour trip to the mall, the park, or whatever interests you. Reconnect, and get in touch with me on what that does for your marriage, and sex life.

Parting Words

Sex is a journey

Your sex life, just like your marriage is a journey and the thing with journeys is that the *journey* is as important as the destination. Likewise, sex should never be about orgasm, though it is an important aspect of sex, the act itself is also important.

One of the lessons I learnt from my late father was that of growth or death. My dad used to say, "anything that doesn't grow, dies". Scientists may pick this apart, but in many cases, this is true. Growth is a part of life, we grow old, we pursue growth in our businesses and careers, and likewise, we ought to pursue growth in our marriages. I like to think of growth in marriage as something that happens over time, but the passage of time does not necessarily translate to growth.

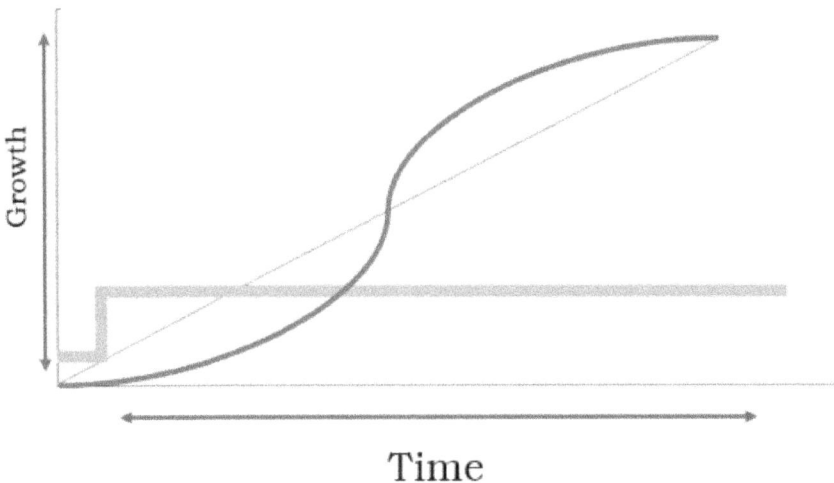

Time

If we consider the diagram above, we will note that growth is an arbitrary output that cannot be measured reliably. But for the purpose of my theory, we would all agree that growth is something intangible, yet we can see it on the basis of outcomes. Our assessment of growth is subjective, and unique to what we consider growth to be. But what is consistent for all of us is that we want to see growth in our relationships. For example, an issue that resulted in fierce argument and strife between you and your spouse in the first year of marriage should reasonably be handled with much more maturity when you have been married 20 years. You can plug in your own examples, but I am sure the point is clear.

Time is a factor we all understand, in the case of this diagram, it refers to the time that a couple has been married. On the one curve in orange, we see that no growth takes place, then sudden growth early on, and then a stagnation for the rest of the marriage. This is where many people who have been married for decades get it wrong; they mistakenly attribute the passage of time to the growth of their marriage. Sadly, if no effort is put into the relationship or any area of it, things will stay the same and you will relive what you have grown to learn for the rest of your life. Assuming that you know more about marriage because you have been with your wife for 30 years is not entirely true, if it were what of a person who was married for 5 years, got arrested for 25 years and their spouse waited for them? Do you suppose the quality of this person's relationship can be compared to another couple who have been married for 30 years? I don't think so, because passage of time alone is not enough to justify a good marriage.

The other two curves seem to have growth over time with some consistency. The difference is the rate of growth. This is down to effort, if you invest in growing yourself and your marriage consistently and vigorously, the results will speak for themselves. You will have a fulfilling marriage and you will come to *know* your spouse deeper with each passing year.

As a person who has been married for less than 5 years, I often get jeers from people who have been married longer than a decade. Some even go so far as to say I was married *'yesterday'*, almost as if they are telling me I know nothing about marriage and I am to learn. In those moments, I have a good mind to keep my mouth shut, because the sad reality of some of their marriages (looking from the outside) is that there is little to no growth. They have the same tendencies that they had when I was growing up right before their eyes. To borrow from the Apostle Paul's advice to Timothy, *do not let any man despise the youth of your marriage*. No matter how long you have been married, your focus should be growing in the knowledge of your spouse and growing intrapersonally because the two are inseparable. You cannot grow as a spouse without you growing as an individual. Lastly, no matter how long you have been married, the scripture says marriage is a mystery. What you think you know is what the Lord has graciously revealed to you, and even then, marriage remains a mystery. None of us 'have it', stay humble and keep learning.

Sex was created by God for our enjoyment in the context of marriage. It is a gateway to deep connection between loving spouses, the result of which is children (sometimes). So just like we cherish all other blessings the LORD gives to us, we ought to cherish sex. We are to strive to serve each other sexually because our spouse's pleasure depends on it. Remember, when you focus on pleasuring your spouse, and they focus on pleasuring you- you will have an explosive sexual experience whose flames will burn till you are called to the LORD.

Great sex is not a destination. There's no *holy grail* with sex, it is a journey which requires both spouses to relish in. To be frank, great sex is something that is couple dependent. My version of this with my wife is different to our other married friends. The idea is to find what works for both of you by communicating this in a loving and constructive manner. And no, the grass is not greener on the other side. You and your spouse have the potential of creating amazing sexual experiences, any challenges to doing so are just there to bring you closer. I suppose that would be the summation of sex- an experience created by God to bring closeness in marriage, emotionally, spiritually and physically. Accept the challenge, and you will benefit from the reward.

Just remember not to try too much too soon. My advice is that you hone in on intimacy, developing the habit of having quality conversations that are uninterrupted and meaningful. It is when you take interest in knowing your spouse that you are likely to increase your frequency of 'knowing' them. Slow is also the fastest that some of us can go, so pace yourself. Much has been covered in this text, but 'Rome was not built in a day', neither will a great sex life. Take it easy, enjoy the journey and you'll be fine.

List of Resources

The resources listed below are not paid advertisements. I have had no prior communication with the individuals responsible the creation of these resources. I simply admire their work, and I've also made use of the information I found there in my own marriage and found it to be helpful. I hope you find value in them too.

- Married Sex: *For Christian Couples*

Possibly the first and only book I have read on Sex that did not give me the irks. This book is written by a counsellor and a pastor, giving perspective on each topic from both points of view. What I appreciated most is the honesty of the authors' coverage of some touchy elements about sex. It is a definite must-have for couples seeking to spice up their sex life. I've personally bought several copies of this book and gifted them to couples in my circle. Just their reaction alone tells you how people in the church deal with the topic of sex- they don't.

- *Christianfriendlysexpositions.com*

This is a site I came across from reading Married Sex. There is a host of sex positions explained in detail and appropriately illustrated in a manner that won't have you repenting in the evening. What I appreciate most about the site is that it doesn't aim to pervert sex like the secular coverage of sex does, instead the aim is to enrich Christian couples with knowledge of the wide variety they have in the realm of sex.

- *5 Love languages*

I got a copy of the book from a friend of mine. I couldn't put it down. The lessons I have taken from it continue to inform my view of communication in marriage. Most times we have disagreements, areas of disappointment and discontentment because of a breakdown in communications. What this book does is to help you understand your love language, as well as your spouse's love language. This way, you have the tools to communicate and receive love more effectively as a couple.

- *Atomic Habits*

This is a bit of a wild card in the context of a Christian book. But what this book has opened my eyes to is the power of habit. Not only in a positive light, but the destructive potential of negative habits. James Clear sets out a framework for building better habits, a skill that is transferrable across all areas of our lives.

- *His Needs, Her Needs*

One of the first books we read on marriage as a couple. The premise of this book is that marriage is an institution of need-satisfaction. Each person satisfying the needs of their spouse. Chief among these is sex for men, and affection for the women. The other key concept of the book is that of the Love bank, and the relating love deposits. Get yourself a copy of this book and work towards satisfying your spouse's needs.

- https://www.ligonier.org/learn/series/intimate-marriage

This is a series about marriage taught by the late Dr R. C. Sproul. In this series, he goes through what intimate marriage is and what makes for an intimate marriage between spouses. There are some valuable insights that are life-giving for a marriage of any state

- Dear Young Married Couple

One of the podcasts I listen to for relevant insights into various topics about marriage. The hosts, Adam and Karissa King, structure the podcast as a dear diary to a young married couple on helpful topics with the aid of their wealth of knowledge from counselling themselves and the guests they bring onto their show. It is an amazing resource to look into for building healthy marriages. They also offer other resources that are worth considering.

- Crazy Little Thing Called Marriage

This is another one of those podcasts that keeps challenging you to be better in marriage. This one is hosts by Greg and Erin Smalley, who are a seasoned couple with decades of experience in helping married couples. They have done such wonderful work for the Kingdom of God in the area of relationships and their advice is worth two listens per episode. It's so funny, but I had been listening to some of their material and heard of them when I was much younger, tuning into some Focus on the Family content aired on a community radio station I used to listen to.

Designing systems that work

Designing your **Sex Life Vision**© is something we spoke about in Chapter 2. Much of the hurdles with designing a vision is the daunting reality of where you are versus where you want to be- the wedge has a way of seeming impossible to bridge. My simple advice is something I often struggle to apply in my own space- understanding the concept that good things taking time. Just remember that you don't have to solve the 'how' today, you just need to know where you want to be.

Accountability sexsystem© – as stated in the introduction, great sex cannot happen outside of a great marriage. And great marriage is not a one-man show... get mentors or befriend other couples... seek help. I implore you send the link to the book to 2 other married couples, and talk about it. I'd also suggest making use of the *Crash Course on Sex Workbook©*. The workbook is not a must have, but it could be useful for those who struggle with intimacy or even knowing what the right questions to tackle as a couple.

Christian Marriage Love Cycle©

In writing this book, I had so much in my heart to share on the subject of married sex. Stuff I have observed in my brief experience in marriage, things I have seen in failed marriages (including my own parent's marriage), and things I have learnt from years of consuming marriage material. However, the greatest of all truths that sits at the heart of this book is this: loving and submitting to each other sacrificially is the most sustainable way to keep a marriage alive. This is obviously not the brain-child of my genius, but the genius of God. In the Apostle Paul's Letter to the Ephesians, we find a command that Husbands should love their wives as Christ loved the church. We also learn that wives ought to submit to their husbands (see Ephesians 5:22-33). It is this inspired writing that I call the genius of God. You see, when a husband loves his wife sacrificially, it causes her to submit to him sacrificially. When a wife submits to her husband sacrificially, it causes him to love her sacrificially. This is the Christian Marriage Love Cycle.

It doesn't matter who starts it, what matters is that both spouses reciprocate what they receive sacrificially. So that the husband who is submitted to owes his wife a debt of love, and a beloved wife owes her husband a debt of submission. I believe that a marriage where the Christian Marriage Love Cycle is made a lifestyle remains strong for life.

The other interesting thing as I tried to put together a coherent body of work on such a vast subject, I realised that love and submission [of self] are inseparable. If we look to the way love is described in 1 Corinthians 13, we note the following about love:

- Love is patient

- Love is kind

- It does not envy or boast

- It is not arrogant

- It does not insist on its own way

There are other descriptions, but let's take these five.

- One cannot subject themselves under someone without needing to exercise patience.

- You cannot submit unless you are kind (which means to show yourself useful and act benevolently).

- Envy and boasting do not co-exist with submission

- Submission, being the subjection of self unto another, and arrogance are mutually exclusive.

- Submission is yielding from your own way and subjecting yourself to that of another.

From the above, we see that one cannot submit without love, nor can anyone love without submission. But who do we submit to? Are husbands supposed to submit to their wives? This isn't what the scripture is saying, rather, a husband submitted to Christ as his Lord will not find it difficult to love his wife. A wife submitted to Christ as her Lord will not find it difficult to submit to her husband, who represents Christ in their marriage. Likewise, a husband who loves and has experienced the love of Christ in his life will not have difficulty loving his wife and a wife who has experienced the same love will love her husband. It is all linked. In the end, we are told to love one another sacrificially, that is putting the other before ourselves.

Confessions of the author

You will remember the mind, body, spirit diagram presented in chapter two. From this diagram, you will note that the contents of this book deals mainly with the mind and body aspects of this trichotomy of our existence. This is not a mistake, the spirit is side-lined as a lesser of the three. In fact, you may deduce that the spirit is littered throughout the pages of this book. We need connection to the spiritual for us to walk by faith, and it is this faith that sustains our marriages. So I did not deal with the spirit directly or specifically because it is a pre-requisite to a successful Christian marriage. In fact, fixing our spirit man has a tendency of spilling over to our mind and body, so the whole being is permeated by the work of **The Spirit** [of God].

I don't claim to have covered it all in this book. I can't possibly, because sex is so vast and uniquely couple-specific. What I have done is provide you a base on which you can both evaluate where you are and build your dream sex life. For example, what many would expect in a book about sex is how to please your man (if you're a woman), or how to last longer (for men). These are some of the fundamental questions that get answered by many writers and contributors in the area of sex. My thought is that there's no point in me telling you how to last longer in something your struggle to even get started in. If you tell a man who has not had sex with his wife in months (and has remained true to his vows throughout) that you can help him last longer in bed, he'd laugh at your face and tell you "just as long as you can tell me how I can get my wife to gimme some". So the purpose here was to give fundamentals, who knows? Maybe in future I just may consider building from this content and giving some strategies for those who would want to become more proficient in sex.

You may read through the pages of this book and write it off as simple, but simple doesn't mean the information is irrelevant or untrue. I'd caution you to do some introspection - if you think the content of this book is simple, ask yourself this question: why do so many people fail to apply it in their lives? Perhaps you're one of those who is struggling to apply simple principles. The truth is that life is not about being or living like a genius, otherwise we'd all be geniuses and I suppose there wouldn't be any genius, technically. Life is about applying *simple* principles consistently and intentionally. Over time, these become your habits. The habits become your character. Your character will determine *who you are* and what your life has been about. So be willing to start small and don't despise humble beginnings.[67]

You may also consider the contents of this book as leaning more into the relationship than sex, that's not coincidence. There is no great sex without a relationship. Sex without a relationship is what casual sex is about, physical contact devoid of any connection.

Finally, this has been a *Crash Course* it is not an exhaustive volume on sex, my advice is that we should all seek out great resources that will inspire us to improving how we serve our spouses (I will give a list of these at the end of this chapter). What you will appreciate about this list is that it appears to have very little about sex, and more about relationships. This is not a mistake, our sexual experience tends to mirror our relationship situation, so when we fix that, the outcome is usually a better sex life.

My writing struggles

There were times during the writing process where I didn't know what to say. Many times where I doubted the necessity of the subject matter of this text, and even the content. What kept me going was the desire to achieve what I had set out to do- which was to write a book to completion. What I also want is to make money and to help someone strengthen their marriage. So many times, marriages go to the ground because of money, but more often than we realise, relationships come to an end because of a lack of harmony on the sexual front. People claim to have "fallen out of love" when in fact their relationally out of tune and their sex life takes a hit because they're not connecting physically, the emotional and spiritual take a hit, and it is the 'chicken and the egg' conundrum all over, until they part.

The roller-coaster of writing this book was filled with moments of Self-doubt, joy, excitement and hope. My hope was that it would become a volume of meaningful lessons on a scary subject. It was exciting to write each word as it brought me closer to a fully articulated version of what I felt the Lord laid in my heart concerning married sex. I really enjoyed the many milestones I had set for myself, most notably the one of writing daily for 31 days: this was a true example of what writing is about, consistency and not volume. I also battled Self-doubt when I hit roadblocks and I questioned why I was doing this in the first place. It was real fun to put together but it was also hard, it challenged me to consider my own sex life and whether I was doing what I as preaching in this book? I also found myself sitting in front of the laptop and doodling; doing everything under the sun but writing. It was tough, but knowing that someone's life and marriage might be enriched by it was truly encouraging. I also had set a deadline with my wife (my editor) that I did not meet, that was bitter sweet, because throughout the writing process, she hadn't had a sniff of what was in the book.

My appeal to you

If you've been blessed by this book, allow me to make this appeal to you once more. Please share a link to this book to another 3 couples of your choosing. Preferably couples who are in your accountability system as discussed in the introduction to this book, i.e. a couple who's been married longer than you, one that was married at relatively the same time as you and a couple whose marriage is younger than yours. I hope your marriage is strengthened as you make a habit of building an ecosystem of accountability around it in this way. I would also like to get some feedback on your experience through this content, so don't hesitate to get in touch with me via email or social media.

The very last thing I would like to ask you is to be an example of a great marriage. Where you are, your marriage is a picture of Christ and the Church, but also a beacon of hope for many who may be struggling in marriage. Be on the lookout for such people. You may think you are struggling, but some people have it much worse. Realise that you are an instrument in the hands of God, let Him use you and your marriage to heal others.

References

Cambridge Dictionary. (2023, feb 3). *English Dictionary*. Retrieved from Cambridge Dictionary: https://dictionary.cambridge.org/dictionary/english

Clear, J. (2018). *Atomic Habits*. London: Penguin Random House UK.

Covenant Eyes. (2020). *Porn Stats: 250+ facts, quotes, and statistics about pornography use (2018 Edition)*. Owosso, Michigan, United States of America: Covenant Eyes. Retrieved May 2023, from www.covenanteyes.com/pornstats/

Evans-Pritchard, B. (2023, August 6). *Works That Work*. Retrieved from Works That Work: https://worksthatwork.com/1/urinal-fly

Oxford Dictionaries. (2023). *Definitions*. Retrieved from Oxford Learners Dictionary: https://www.oxfordlearnersdictionaries.com/

Pascal, B. (1958). *Pascal's Pensees*. New York: E.P. Dutton & Co., INC. Retrieved May 4, 2023, from https://www.gutenberg.org/files/18269/18269-h/18269-h.htm

Priest, R. J. (2001). Missionary Positions: Christian, Modernist, Postmodernist. *The University of Chicago Press Journals*.

Sproul, R. Y. (2023, February 8). Knowing Each Other. United States of America: Ligonier Ministries.

Strong, J. (1890). Strong's Exhaustive Concordance of the Bible. Abingdon Press.

Index

L

M

O

P

Q

R

S

---

[1] This is my favourite movie

[2] *You* = target audience

[3] Here, as in all other places in this book, I make the assumption that the reader is a Christian and views life from a lens of biblical principles.

[4] Body count is a term floated to represent the number of people one has had sex with in the past. For example, if I had sexual relations with 10 women prior to my wife my *body count* would be 10, regardless of the number of times I had relations with each of those 10 women. This becomes more interesting as people would prefer to have sex with their 'ex' rather than a stranger to 'keep the *body count* under control'.

[5] The church here is not the brick-and-mortar church, but the body of Christ at large.

[6] The spiritual elements of sex are sufficiently preached about- purity, soul ties, the list is endless. I will not be going into this in this book.

[7] More on how to tend to your spouse's emotions is littered across this book. Fret not.

[8] Some may argue that stress and grief are a wonderful backdrop for highly charged sex. I've read about and experienced this, just remember to never use your spouse as a means to an end. Enjoy sex with love and as a service to the other.

[9] https://open.spotify.com/episode/2Aom8vXhsAtuqGv9Yjs2iw

[10] Having a specified time, and a word or phrase that only the two of you know is another means of adding individuality to your 'sacred' moment and fun.

[11] I talk about skills transfer in *Chapter 11*, this is an example of transferring knowledge and skill from your vocation into your sex life.

[12] I know you Christian people will use Sarah and Abraham as an example of how bearing kids after 70-years of age is possible. But let's not test God, but let us take the opportunities we have at the appropriate time.

[13] I have not read any of these myself, but I have heard of them. These are sometimes rooted in spiritual practices that are less than Godly. If you choose to read them, do so at your own risk.

[14] By thrust, I mean the force of pushing your penis into the vagina, and strokes mean the speed at which this is done.

[15] I contemplated using the word "watching" and realised that there are a number of ways that one can take in pornographic content; there's text, image, motion pictures, and even audio... So consuming works better.

[16] Married Sex in this context refers to sex in the institution of marriage. This is a rather general application than a specific one.

[17] www.covenanteyes.com

[18] Do to others what you would have them do to you... this is the golden rule.

[19] Salute to the loving mothers out there, you are awesome. Seeing my wife and how she tends to my son makes me appreciate my own mom even more.

[20] Some may argue, with good reason that sex is about procreation. Whether this be the primary or secondary reason can be debated. What is not debatable is that neither side of the argument can claim that performance is superior to procreation nor pleasure.

[21] In Chapter 9, I share some experiences on a 30-day sex challenge we did with my wife. More on it later. On day 20 of the streak, we changed location and had some 'provisions' for spillages. This made us both free to let loose and we realised how not being prepared in that area can cause mental blockages and keep you from fully experiencing the pleasure of climax.

[22] Appropriate language is subjective. Your appropriate is likely different to mine, however, there are basics, like the fact that you wouldn't call your wife a derogatory term just because you're in the heat of the moment.

[23] A bit more coverage on exercise and sex could be found in chapter 10.

[24] We were so tired on our wedding night that sex was not even a possibility. We dosed off, but this is my version of the story, so take it with a grain of salt #wink.

[25] There are a variety of options to choose from. Water-based or silicone lubricants are typically the two criteria to choose from. Water-based lubricants are known to slow sperm motility, so consider this if pregnancy is your aim. Silicone lubricants are great for longer sessions where extended lubrication is necessary to see you through the act. So it is good to experiment with a few and find one that works for both of you.

[26] Seeking support for mental health issues is usually neglected among men. But my observations indicate to me that we are the ones who spend more time 'in our heads'. This behaviour can get out of hand really quickly if it is to go unchecked. Personally, I have a cousin-brother who committed suicide, the image of his lifeless body always brings a rush of questions to my mind. Chiefly, I wonder what could I have contributed to remedy whatever situation plaguing his mind? Moral of the story: seek help, it is okay to not be okay. It is not okay to be okay with not being okay.

[27] Some sexual fetishes involve the excrement of human waste onto and into another. This is inhuman and debases the other person. It is not something to be found among the children of God.

[28] I don't mean to re-write scripture here, but bring an understanding of how the delight-desire framework of God works.

[29] And Jesus said, "Father, forgive them, for they know not what they do..." (Luke 23:34 ESV)

[30] This is all the personal information I am at liberty to share. Everything is seen by me through the experiences of others. Here and everywhere else in this book (#jokes, lol)

[31] If the tips given here are a bit much for your schedule, why not try outsourcing/automating them, like getting a laundry service, cleaning service, setting reminders to shower, brush your teeth, or investing in an aqua flosser. The idea is to remove the hassle from doing these things.

[32] Habit Stacking is a concept borrowed from the writing of James Clear in *Atomic Habits*- a must read for personal development.

[33] No disrespect to Mr. Putin, I grew up watching the news with my dad and I always wondered if that man sang or danced. Please do not take this to be political commentary, it's simply an observation. If you're Russian, give me grace, we have had a president who sings and dances when he engages with the public.

[34] Interestingly, of the 4 elements (fire, wind, earth and water), fire seems to be the one that can be quenched by the other three when given sufficient quantities.

[35] At this point, I'm sure this sounds more like a business proposition than a sex manual. But trust the process.

[36] This changed after our son was born... motherhood, hey #sigh

[37] I was born and raised in the Republic of South Africa, not to be confused with Southern Africa or the South of Africa, the continent.... Though that is where my country is geographically.

[38] The craziness of this expectation was my disregard for my own humanity; I too get tired, there are other factors that may get in the way like an emergency, a work trip, or even a sick child. I was so fixated on having and using my 'licence' to have sex that I forgot that it required some preconditions to be met.

[39] 2 hours x 365.25 days = 730.5 hours.... **730.5 hours ÷ 24 hours = 30.4375 days**, which amounts to roughly a month.

[40] Check out the resources chapter for references to some of my most profound readings on this subject of love languages.

[41] *Churchianity* is a spin on the word Christianity. It is a term used to refer to an outward appearance of faith in Christ but an inward deficiency of the true faith. It is when supposed Christians place emphasis on church rules more than the will of God through His word. It is a false sense of belonging to Christ when 'He does not know you'.

[42] Typical of us Christians to see the bright side of everything, including a pandemic. As an aside, my bestie's mom is a nurse, and she was remarking on the sudden rise of births following the lockdowns, she jokingly commented that 'people were busy' during those times.

[43] Check out any video of Creed 3 on chemistry test.

[44] If you plan out time for sex, I would suggest giving this slot a name, something that only you two can know. This adds a bit of humour to the experience, and further fans the flames of connection as you are the only two people who know what you're talking about.

[45] This was from October 2019 – February 2021, when we moved into our new home. We stopped because our shower and tub were too small.

[46] The Five Love Languages: The Secret to Love that Lasts by Gary Chapman

[47] His Needs, Her Needs – Building an affair-proof marriage by Willard F. Harley

[48] The fact that this was on-going through the Passover weekend was no help. I was involved in helping out at my church and this required quite a bit of physical exertion. Alas, the challenge had to continue, and we were benefitting.

[49] By extra-marital I am referring to anything outside of marriage

[50] More on this in the Parting words Chapter, interesting resources are listed for your consideration.

[51] See *Parting Words* chapter on the 5 Love Languages to learn how best to communicate love and affection to your spouse.

[52] The fact of consent and willingness from both parties goes without saying here. However, I am yet to find a man who would say 'no' to his wife's call to sex. Not without good reason, and even that has to be better than "I don't feel like it".

[53] Much of the sexual literature out there refers to ejaculation/orgasm as 'coming', which is not to be mistaken for coming, i.e. coming home.

[54] Note that needs change as we evolve and our preferences change. This is normal, and it normalises our need to stay connected. We need different inputs to our lives in different seasons, so stay connected.

[55] Once you realise that your time is a commodity, you will understand that what you spend your time on has to provide decent value in return. Time spent in the gym has to yield a higher value outcome than what has been sacrificed to be in the gym (i.e. leisure vs. healthy body). Are you trading your time for things that bring value to your life, or stuff that sucks the life out of you?

[56] This automatically eliminates threesomes and orgies.

[57] Our OBGYN had given strict instructions before discharging my wife after labour: **NO SEX FOR 6 WEEKS!!!**

[58] I avoided using the word 'distraction' or a derivative of the same, because children are anything but. I do not conform to the standards of this world, where more people are choosing to be single and child-free because children are so "distracting". Be reminded that one of the earliest commands given to man by God is that we are to be fruitful and multiply.

[59] Credit does not equal glory in this instance. I'm aware of how touchy Christians can get about taking God's glory. Saints, it is the Lord that gives us strength to do life, but we still have to make use of the strength we are given, here is where the credit becomes ours. Even though the wise use of the strength is given by grace.

[60] This is where abstinence before marriage pays dividends because you have done it before, it doesn't seem like death to go for 6 weeks without sex, or even longer. Your love for your wife won't vanish in the process.

[61] One example of this is the very book you're reading. I've struggled so much to get it written because I wanted it to be perfect; badly so. But I have since realised that I am learning, and I am confident that it has value for the reader and is worth sharing. I hope you are blessed by it and that your marriage is enriched by your reading of it.

[62] See Chapter 9 on the 30 sex challenge

[63] A blocker is a person or thing that blocks you from enjoying sex.

[64] This doesn't exempt us from challenges in life. Jesus said we would have tribulation in this earth, but generally, when God blesses us, we do not experience sorry.

[65] The idea of my father making stipulations over the life of his grandson may sound foreign to some, but in African culture it is customary for seniors in the family to lay down rules for their own families. So that even when I get married, my father has the right to make stipulations on how we ought to do things in the family.

[66] It may seem out-of-place to talk about isolation in a sex book, but the idea that a great relationship is correlated to a great sex life justifies the inclusion.

[67] One of the local banks in South Africa once used the tag line "simplicity is the ultimate sophistication", this is so true in the context of applying simple truths in life.

Don't miss out!

Visit the website below and you can sign up to receive emails whenever S. S. Thabethe publishes a new book. There's no charge and no obligation.

https://books2read.com/r/B-A-TOGAB-HXNNC

BOOKS 2 READ

Connecting independent readers to independent writers.

About the Author

S. S. Thabethe is passionate about family and marriage. He believes that a healthy marriage is at the heart of fulfilled families. His greatest joy, second to being a Child of God by salvation in Jesus Christ, is being a husband and a father. He believes that these roles are the greatest roles in which he can imitate Christ and God the Father. Writing, reading and speaking are lifelong passions of his through which he has been favoured by God to experience His goodness. He resides in Durban, South Africa with his loving wife and their very energetic little boy. Trained to be a Chartered Accountant (CPA), he has a keen interest in academia and aspires to follow in his father's footsteps and obtain his 'Ph.D.'

9 798223 546573